THE
GREAT
DISSENTERS

BY THE AUTHOR

Commemorative Stamps of the U.S.A.
They Almost Made It
Trappers of the West
The Great Dissenters

THE GREAT DISSENTERS

*Guardians of Their Country's
Laws and Liberties*

BY FRED REINFELD

Thomas Y. Crowell Company · New York

ACKNOWLEDGMENT

The author is most grateful to Thomas Dutelle and his able staff at the East Meadow Public Library for their gracious and persevering efforts in furnishing research material for this book.

Manufactured in the United States of America by the Vail-Ballou Press, Inc., Binghamton, New York
LIBRARY OF CONGRESS CATALOG CARD No. 59-12502
Second Printing

INTRODUCTION

A story about Lord Melbourne, the first Prime Minister of Queen Victoria's reign, reports that he used to tell his Cabinet: "I don't care what we say, but we'd better all say the same thing."

The six Americans who are described in this book were all contemporaries of Lord Melbourne; but they had convictions and were not afraid to express them; nor did they set any store by saying the same things that everyone else was saying. Adams was a statesman who put justice ahead of re-election. Emerson was a philosopher who prided himself on having no disciples, for he wanted men to think for themselves, not like himself. Mann was a reformer who preached tirelessly that the life of a democracy depends on the education it provides for its citizens. Garrison, another reformer, was regarded as a freak because he was outraged by the presence of slavery in a free country. Thoreau, undiscouraged by the commercial failure of his books, serenely continued to write to please his own taste. Holmes courageously dissented from many Supreme Court decisions over a period of three decades.

As we read about the lives of these men, we see that our own age is not the only one that has had a powerful surge toward uniformity: the age of Emerson had its equivalent of Organization Men and men in gray flannel suits. Yet these great dissenters are recognized today as great Americans precisely because they dared to be themselves.

Contents

Contents

What can be said to be permanent in this fleeting world, if not our remembrance of the deeds of great men?

—LUDWIG BAUER

JOHN QUINCY
ADAMS

A stout heart and a clear conscience, and never despair.

Of all our great Americans, John Quincy Adams is the least appreciated and the most misunderstood. The reason for this may be that while he was a great American, he was in many ways a very untypical American.

Adams, for example, was the only President's son who ever became President. He was, in fact, the only President's son who achieved distinction by his own efforts.

The sons of famous men rarely rise above mediocrity —perhaps because from early childhood the father's preeminence is constantly impressed on them, until they lose all hope of becoming equally great. But John Quincy Adams was different—it was his destiny to be always "different"—and while he venerated his father, he had a burning ambition to be worthy of his father, of his family, of his country.

1

Actually, Adams had three notable careers: as a diplomat in his country's service; as President; and, in his old age, as a crusader against slavery. He was born in 1767, nine years before the appearance of the Declaration of Independence, and he died in 1848, thirteen years before the outbreak of the Civil War. Thus his lifetime spanned some of the most exciting years of American history, and he played a leading role in many of the important events of that age.

While still a comparatively young man, Adams served as United States Minister to Holland, Prussia, and Russia. These were trying assignments during the agitated years of the Napoleonic wars in Europe, when the infant American republic was contemptuously buffeted by France and England as a by-product of their life-and-death struggle. The United States was fortunate to be represented in those humiliating years by Adams with dignity, firmness, integrity, and outstanding ability.

Toward the end of the War of 1812, Adams was appointed one of the commissioners to represent his country in the difficult and almost endless peace negotiations with Great Britain. Here again Adams rendered an invaluable service to his country by his uncompromising stand for American rights. After the defeat of Napoleon, the British held all the military trumps and were in a position to divert large forces toward the New World. Consequently their negotiators took a high-handed tone, so that it required all of Adams' determination, strength of character, and patriotic wisdom to hold out for reasonably satisfactory peace terms.

After peace was concluded, Adams was named Ameri-

to read is something of a mystery; but of this passion there can be no doubt. Thus, we find him writing in 1839:

"There is such seduction in a library of good books that I cannot resist the temptation to luxuriate in reading; and, because I have so much to write, I count all time lost that is not spent in writing."

His passion for writing went hand in hand with that of reading. To it we owe the great diary which he kept for sixty years, and which is unrivaled in the field of American historical memoirs. In this fascinating journal Adams recorded the hopes, the aspirations, and the resentments which he was too reserved to express to his fellow men. But this was only a small part of his output. It will take historians many years to master all the letters, speeches, articles, pamphlets, and private papers that streamed from his pen.

Adams was ahead of his time in realizing the importance of the natural sciences. Not only did he take an amateur's deep delight in science; he anticipated some of the most grueling problems of our own day in his insistence that the federal government must play an active role in promoting scientific investigation. How modern the following statement of 1843 sounds!

"The people of this country do not sufficiently estimate the importance of patronizing and promoting science as a principle of political action."

It is to Adams, by the way, that we owe the establishment of the Smithsonian Institution after a ten-year, single-handed struggle against mocking opposition.

Above all, Adams was a deeply religious man. For years he got up before dawn in order to have time to read the Bible for an hour. He read through the Old and New Testaments consecutively, and when he was finished, he started all over again. He read all the versions, in foreign languages as well as in English, that he could lay his hands on. He compared texts, studied the commentators, compared their conclusions.

The result was that his political views were deeply colored by his religious convictions. Thus, despite his fiercely patriotic love for his country, he could not agree with Stephen Decatur's famous toast: "Our country: in her intercourse with foreign nations may she always be in the right; but our country, right or wrong."

Adams modified Decatur's toast in this way: "Our country, right or wrong. I disclaim all patriotism incompatible with the principles of eternal justice."

Adams expressed the same thought in different words when he wrote to a friend, "Truth, virtue, honour, the dignity of human nature, are the touchstones by which the conduct of nations as well as individuals is to be tested." Adams not only believed this; he tried to live up to it.

What kind of influences made Adams the sort of man he was?

From his earliest childhood years he was subjected to pressure—affectionate, wise, tactful pressure, but pressure all the same—to put forth his best efforts, to achieve, to excel. Everything he did, even into his fifties and sixties, he dutifully subjected to his parents' careful and generally approving scrutiny.

It is no wonder that under such constant supervision, Adams turned into a severely self-critical man. Others found him hardheaded, humorless, opinionated, harsh in expression, unwilling to go to any trouble to please others. Family affection had been ingrained into his character so deeply that friendliness to outsiders was correspondingly weakened.

The following entry, written in 1812, is typical of Adams' pitilessly self-critical attitude:

"I am forty-five years old. Two-thirds of a long life are past and I have done nothing to distinguish it by usefulness to my country or mankind."

If Adams could write with such sweeping unfairness about himself, how would he judge the shortcomings of other people? Here is a characteristic comment, written during the peace negotiations at Ghent in Belgium in 1814 about the other American commissioners:

"They sit after dinner and drink bad wine and smoke cigars, which neither suits my habits nor my health, and absorbs time which I cannot spare. I find it impossible, even with the most rigorous economy of time, to do half the writing I ought."

Adams was particularly annoyed at Henry Clay, and there is a delightfully half-comic, half-sour description of Clay, after an all-night session of card-playing, going to bed at the same time that Adams gets up to read the Bible! And yet Adams had to admit that he and Clay shared the same bad qualities: "There is the same dogmatical, overbearing manner, the same harshness of look and expression, and the same forgetfulness of the courtesies of society in both."

Such entries as this one (London, 1816) appear again and again in Adams' diary:

"I said two or three silly things to Sir James Mackintosh, and was altogether stiff and dull beyond my usual measure."

And three years later, at the height of his fame as Secretary of State, he writes in despair:

"I am a man of reserved, cold, austere, and forbidding manners: my political enemies say, a gloomy misanthropist, and my personal enemies, an unsocial savage. With a knowledge of the actual defect in my character, I have not the pliability to reform it."

Many years later, when he has mellowed considerably, he is still abashed by the enthusiastic applause of a friendly audience and by "a highly complimentary address, which I answered as best I could, in a speech full of inanity and gratitude, shamefaced and awkward, as I must always be in answering compliments to myself."

There is something very touching about the painfully roundabout way in which Adams was eventually recognized as a great American. Early training taught him to do the right thing, indifferent to popular approval and hardened to public criticism.

And yet, as the distinguished son of one of the Founding Fathers, he was deeply respected for the magnificent work he had done in protecting American interests abroad. His integrity, his sincere patriotism, and his scholarly breadth of mind all set him apart from the general run of politicians; in fact these qualities only enhanced the awe with which he was regarded. As a fighter second to none, he commanded the reluctant admiration of his enemies.

Thus, John Quincy Adams, who never courted popular favor, eventually won the esteem of his fellow citizens. Deeply gratified as he must have been, Adams nevertheless could not dispel the attitudes of a lifetime. His best efforts had met with criticism, misunderstanding, ridicule, reproach, and even slander; for these reactions he had always been prepared—sometimes philosophically prepared and sometimes miserably prepared. But when he at last received the popular esteem and affection for which he had always unknowingly longed, he was wholly unprepared.

After all, what was this America for which Adams had given sixty years of his life? Was it only the grand slogans of the Revolution which had fired his soul, was it only an abstraction of paper documents and a system of law? No, this America was his fellow citizens, his fellow Americans, for whose welfare he had labored untiringly and unceasingly, whose happiness meant more to him than anything else in the world. And so, when he had unmistakable signs of their gratitude at last, the "Old Man Eloquent," as he had been affectionately nicknamed, could only be "shamefaced and awkward."

John Quincy Adams was the exceptional son of exceptional parents. His mother, Abigail Adams, was one of the most remarkable women of her day—highly intelligent, witty, self-educated, yet affectionate and with a woman's genius for creating happiness in the family circle. She impressed on her oldest son that he was to be "a guardian of his country's laws and liberties."

To the young boy, the American Revolution was almost an Adams family activity. His father, John Adams, was one of the most distinguished of the Founding Fathers. It was John Adams' idea that George Washington should command the American forces. The immortal words of the Declaration of Independence had a special meaning for John Quincy Adams; hadn't his father had a hand in revising the final draft before it was given to the world?

From his father, who was to become the second President of the United States, young Adams learned political sagacity and acquired a mature understanding of men's political passions. It was his father who introduced him to the great and the near-great; his father who, as we would say today, "showed him the ropes" in the world of government. When he was barely in his teens, John Quincy was being guided and advised by Thomas Jefferson and Benjamin Franklin. A few years later, President Washington was marking out the young man for a brilliant career. While still in his twenties, young Adams sent back diplomatic reports to Washington with passages so impressive that the President was glad to adapt them for his Farewell Address.

As the oldest child in the Adams family, John Quincy was trained from the start to a position of distinction and responsibility. When he was eight years old, his mother took him to a spot from which he could safely

watch the Battle of Bunker Hill. All the stirring events
of the opening days of the Revolution in Massachusetts
made an unforgettable impression on the child's mind,
filling him with a patriotic fervor which remained just
as glowing when he was a man of eighty.

With all their deep affection, his parents had no
thought of pampering him. When he was nine years
old he was assigned to take the family mail on horse-
back from Braintree to Boston—a round trip of eighteen miles. During the next two years he twice accompanied his father on diplomatic missions to Europe.
At the age of fifteen, far away from his father, John
Quincy was already fulfilling an assignment of trust and
responsibility as secretary of the United States mission
to Russia.

Journeys that now take a few hours by plane, then
took a month or more by stagecoach, and were often
full of danger. The youngster crossed Europe by himself, and then returned at the age of sixteen to become
his father's private secretary for three years. More than
once he was present when history was being made.

All these unusual experiences left their mark on the
boy. But equally important was the New England background of Puritanism. We see it in the mingling of his
religious and political thinking, and his early resolve to
stick to his convictions no matter how painful the cost.
We see it in the quotation from Voltaire that starts the
famous diary: *"La mollesse est douce et sa suite est
cruelle"* (Laziness is delightful, but its consequences are
disastrous).

All his life he was true to the Puritan ethic of stern

duty and hard work. Time-wasting horrified him, and, as we have seen, he reproached himself for the delightful hours spent with fine books.

It was a lesson constantly reinforced by his solicitous mother. When he was thirteen she wrote him a letter with this characteristic sentence:

"Great necessities call out great virtues" and "form the character of the Hero and Statesman." Here she was echoing William Bradford, who had written more than a century earlier, "All great & honourable actions are accompanied with great difficulties, and must be both enterprised and overcome with answerable courages." It is the heroic sentiment that maintained the faith of the Puritans in their struggle for political and religious liberty, creating a tradition that endured for centuries. This tradition was to give Adams the strength, sixty years later, to press his lone fight in Congress against the infamous Gag Rule, while hostile Congressmen pressed thickly around him and snarled insults at him and bellowed in vain to drown out his shrill attacks on slavery.

John Quincy Adams had learned his lesson well. Again and again one can turn to his parents' affectionate letters to find passages that left their mark on him. Thus, when he was in England and working on the Jay Treaty, which he knew would arouse a storm of disapproval in the United States, his mother wrote him:

"You have put your hand to the plow, and I know you too well to believe or even wish you to look back or shrink from your duty however arduous or dangerous the task assigned to you. You will prove yourself the genuine scion of the stock from which you spring."

By the time young John Quincy was seventeen, he had met many of the famous men of his day—not only Americans, but Frenchmen and Englishmen as well. He spent many happy hours with Thomas Jefferson, then American Ambassador to France. "Spent the evening with Mr. Jefferson whom I love to be with," reads a typical diary entry of the time.

In the course of his studies, John Quincy mastered Latin and Greek; his excellent command of French proved valuable to him throughout his subsequent diplomatic career, and his knowledge of Spanish, German, and Dutch was also helpful. Meanwhile his father taught him algebra, plane and solid geometry, trigonometry, and even some calculus. Despite his Puritan background he indulged his passion for theater and opera to the full. In London he listened enthralled to Pitt, Fox, Sheridan, Burke and other great speakers in Parliament and modeled his own oratorical style on theirs. Years later, though he always disparaged his speaking abilities, he was to be known as the "Old Man Eloquent." The speeches that have come down to us prove that it was a title he well deserved.

A diplomatic career was exciting, but young Adams was level-headed enough to realize that he needed a systematic education. He returned to the United States and completed his formal studies at Harvard, where he extended his reading far beyond the requirements of the curriculum. His temperament and background must have set him apart from the other students, judging from this recollection written more than fifty years later:

"I have throughout my life had an utter aversion to all pageants and public dinners, and never attended one when I could decently avoid it. I was a student at Cambridge when, on the 17th of June, 1786, Charles River Bridge was opened. The colleges were emptied on that day of the students, who flocked to witness the procession and the pageant. I passed the day in the solitude of my study, and dined almost alone in the hall."

His senior oration on "The Importance and Necessity of Public Faith to the Well Being of a Nation," delivered in 1787 when he was twenty, has a pompous ring. The fact is that even then he was an unusually patriotic and well-informed young man, deeply concerned for the fate of his beloved country.

Young Adams saw that the fervent patriotism of the Revolution was dying out and being replaced by the selfish desire of each individual to feather his own nest. War veterans were disillusioned and cynical; fiercely partisan parties were crystallizing to interpret the national interest to their own advantage.

Young Adams, "the man of my whole country," realized that peacetime required its own brand of steady, clear-eyed love of country. He was well aware, as few people are, that peacetime problems are just as pressing, if less colorful and less exciting, than wartime crises which are obvious to all. The nobility of his thinking and his sensitive awareness of the vexing problems that faced the young republic impressed his elders.

While he studied law for three years, he still kept up his wide reading. Nor did he neglect parties, dinners, dances, and other social pleasures. Though pictured as a somber, even dour, man, he had on occasion a sly sense of humor that peers out from his diary, as in this passage written in his sixties:

"The art of making love, muffled up in furs, in the open air, with the thermometer at Zero, is a Yankee invention, which requires a Yankee poet to describe."

And this unusual touch of genial self-revelation is borne out by Copley's portrait of Adams at the age of twenty-eight. It shows him as a very attractive young man, with handsome, sensitive features, lively dark eyes, a good-humored expression, and a hint of a smile playing about his lips.

The outbreak of the French Revolution divided American opinion for and against the overturn and the violence which followed it. The United States had already become the battleground of two violently opposed parties, the Federalists and the Republicans. The Federalists, led by Alexander Hamilton and John Adams, were predominantly the party of the prosperous, the well-born, and those who saw eye to eye with them. They believed in a strongly centralized government. Their opponents, the Republican Party, led by Thomas Jefferson, were the party of the small farmers and ordinary citizens.

They distrusted a strongly centralized government, which they feared might become an instrument of tyranny.

The Republicans believed in strict interpretation of the Constitution. Congress, to their way of thinking, could only pass the kind of laws specifically listed in the Constitution. The Federalists insisted just as vehemently on the doctrine of implied powers. For the Constitution, after listing the fields over which Congress had authority, had added that "the Congress shall have power . . . to make all laws which shall be necessary and proper for carrying into execution the foregoing powers and all other powers vested by this Constitution in the Government of the United States, or in any department or officer thereof." Since this provision is both sweeping and vague, it has led to some of the bitterest battles in American history.

The difference between the two parties has been wittily summed up in this way: the Republicans thought they were as good as anybody else; the Federalists thought they were better than anybody else.

John Quincy Adams, like his father, was a Federalist and took a deep interest in the developing struggle. But he was never a strict party man from the start. To him, "the man of my whole country," the factional spirit was a menace that might some day smash the sacred Union by civil war. The Federalists, passionately devoted to solid, stable government, were terrified by the unsettling tendencies of the French Revolution and the Reign of Terror. They had had their fill of revolution, and wanted orderly processes and secure protection of property. The Republicans, on the other hand, welcomed the overturn in France and saw it as a progressive step that would bring liberty to the French people.

Just at this fateful moment John Quincy Adams was removed from the American scene. For President Washington was so pleased with the young man's able defense of presidential policies that he appointed him Minister to Holland in 1794, when Adams was only twenty-seven. What made the appointment all the more remarkable was that in the troubled state of international affairs, the post required a man of outstanding judgment, delicacy, and firmness. The Continent was in ferment, France and England were waging a "cold war," and the United States was caught in the crossfire of conflicting national ambitions.

Despite his youth and inexperience, young Adams was brilliantly successful. In his negotiations he was patient, prudent, and adroit. Soon his success was rewarded with new ministerial appointments, first to Portugal and then to Prussia, where his achievements were equally creditable.

Meanwhile, momentous events were taking place at home. After serving two terms as President, Washington retired, and in 1796 John Adams was elected President. The war spirit against France was being whipped up by the Federalist followers of Hamilton. As for President Adams, he was naturally opposed, as a good Federalist, to the regime in power in France. But he was also a good American, and he felt that war would be disastrous for his country. Consequently, he came to a peaceful understanding with the French government, though he knew that this statesmanlike and truly patriotic action was political suicide. To him, as later, to his son, the welfare of the country meant more than career and personal glory.

In 1797 Adams married Louisa Johnson, the daughter of an American Consul in London. They had three sons, one of whom, Charles Francis, became the third Adams to render distinguished service to the United States in a time of crisis. For during the Civil War Charles Francis Adams served as Minister to Great Britain, and it was mainly owing to his skillful diplomacy that Great Britain refrained from extending recognition to the Confederacy. Later Charles Francis Adams played a leading role in political reform movements.

When President Adams ran for re-election in 1800, the disappointed Federalists took revenge by refusing to vote for him. He was overwhelmingly defeated and retired permanently from public life. It was a shattering blow for his son. The father had practiced what he had preached; he had put country before personal considerations. It was an example that John Quincy Adams always held before him whenever he had to choose an unpopular course.

Soon the young man retired from the diplomatic service. In 1803 he was elected Senator from Massachusetts by the Federalists. It was on this occasion that he made it clear that he was "the man of my whole country" and would vote for the country's best interests as he saw them, regardless of the position taken by New England or the Federalists. A brutal test of his attitude arrived sooner than anyone had expected.

When President Jefferson bought the huge Louisiana Territory from France, the Federalists roared with rage. After their fierce defense of implied powers, they now claimed that Jefferson lacked the authority to make the purchase. And Jefferson, once the eloquent defender of strict interpretation of the Constitution, took over the old position of the Federalists!

The explanation of this double turnabout was simple enough. New England had played a leading role in the Revolution and in the affairs of the young republic. The Senators and Congressmen from the New England states were all Federalists and consequently opposed to Jefferson's policies. They realized that as new states were carved out of the immense Louisiana Territory, New England would dwindle in importance. And they foresaw that the backwoodsmen and farmers of these new states would favor the Republican Party.

Only one New England member dissented: John Quincy Adams. He took his stand on purely patriotic grounds—the purchase was good for his country, therefore he favored it. And, despite the fury of his fellow Federalists, he courageously stood his ground.

One enraged Federalist sneered that young Adams was "like a kite without a tail." Another exclaimed, "Curse on the young stripling, how he apes his sire." Like his father, young Adams fearlessly staked his career on a principle. He was sincere; the other members of his party covered their partisan interests with high-sounding generalities. No wonder they were furious. When the vote on the ratification of the Purchase came up in the Senate, all the Republicans voted for it. All the Federalists from New England, with one exception, voted against it. Adams voted with the Republicans. The accusations of "Turncoat!" and "Traitor!" wounded him deeply, but they could not make him vote against his patriotic convictions. Like his father, he had apparently committed political suicide.

A few years later Adams was confronted with an even more disagreeable decision. England and France had consistently plundered American commerce, and England had made matters worse by seizing thousands of American seamen on the high seas. The New England Federalists complacently accepted England's policy, for France was still their special hate, and New England merchants and shipowners did profitable business with England. But Adams, ever zealous for his country's honor, was outraged by the actions of Britain's navy. Once more he stood alone against the fury of the New England Federalists.

President Jefferson knew that his puny forces could not fight back. So he resorted to peaceful weapons; in October, 1807, the Republican-controlled Congress passed an act prohibiting all American ships from leaving American harbors. In this way, Jefferson hoped, England would be brought to her senses. Deprived of American goods, she would see the error of her ways.

The crisis filled Adams with anguish. He well knew that the Embargo would bring ruin to New England businessmen and unemployment to New England working people. It was one of those fateful issues that offer no convenient solution. To continue on the previous basis at the dubious mercy of the British navy, would reduce the United States to almost a colonial status and force the conclusion that all the fruits of the Revolution must be lost. For Adams, with his glowing patriotism, such degradation would be too galling. Better to accept a harsh law that would hurt the United States more than England, rather than forfeit precious independence. So, with a heavy heart and fully aware of the hardships that would be visited on his native region, Adams voted for the Embargo. Once more he was the only New England Federalist to vote with the Republicans.

This time Adams unloosed a storm of savage indignation that did not quiet for decades. (In fact, Henry Adams published his great work, *The History of the United States from 1801 to 1817,* eighty years later, primarily to justify his grandfather's courageous action.)

The Federalists did not have to wait long for their revenge. Adams' senatorial term was due to expire in March, 1809. Yet in June, 1808, the Federalist-controlled legislature elected James Lloyd to succeed Adams as Senator from Massachusetts. (United States Senators have been elected by popular vote only since 1913; before that they were elected by state legislatures.)

This action was intended as a rebuke and an insult; and Adams took it as such. Too proud to serve as a discredited "lame-duck," he immediately resigned. At the age of forty-one, with more than twenty years of government service behind him, Adams was through. His public career was ended; no man could recover from this crushing humiliation.

To have the epithet "Benedict Arnold!" hurled at him; to be unceremoniously shoved aside into inglorious ob-

scurity—such were the heartbreaking rewards of being
"the man of my whole country." Or so it seemed; so it
might have been for anyone not gifted with the fighting
spirit of John Quincy Adams.

James Madison, who had been Jefferson's Secretary
of State, was elected President in 1808. As a man of
scholarly tastes and philosophic temperament, Madison
had little use for the party feuds of his day. When he
offered John Quincy Adams the post of Minister to
Russia in 1809, Adams returned to the diplomatic service once more. The Republicans were glad to use him,
the Federalists were happy to have him out of the
country.

During his years in Russia, Adams built up a cordial
relationship with the Czarist regime which was to prove
very useful to the North during the Civil War many
years later. Gradually Adams' position improved. With
the outbreak of the War of 1812 the Federalist Party
was so discredited because of its policy of friendship for
England that its disappearance from the political scene
was certain.

Adams came to be regarded as a member of the Republican Party, though he insisted on maintaining his
independent position. His services as peace commissioner
toward the end of the War of 1812 and as Ambassador
to England were so outstanding that when James Monroe
became President in 1817, he brought Adams back to
Washington as his Secretary of State. (Monroe, as Madison's Secretary of State and Adams' immediate superior,
had worked closely with Adams for years and had the
deepest respect for his abilities.)

So, after leaving the country almost in a state of disgrace, Adams was back in the capital, holding the second most important office in the government, with reasonable prospects of becoming President! For in those days the position of Secretary of State was regarded as the logical steppingstone to the presidency.

It cannot be said that Adams cut a very attractive figure. He was rather short (five feet seven), and the slimness of youth had been transformed into ungainly stoutness. Almost complete baldness made his appearance even more unimpressive. Too much reading had given him an ailment of chronic tearing of the eyes. Spending several hours a day in writing afflicted him with writer's cramp which hardly ever left his hand. In fact, as an old man he had to use a prop for his writing hand.

At social functions Adams was a miserable failure. He dressed poorly, and the art of talking gracefully about trifles was a mystery to him. He was touchy, and had no skill in concealing his irascibility and fits of anger. In small gatherings, as we know, he could be a charming companion; but in a crowd or at a large party he was shy, gruff, and ill at ease.

He found little stimulation in the atmosphere of Washington, which was depressing even in a physical sense. A Massachusetts Congressman of the time described the capital as a "miserable desert" and for good measure he added that "the first appearance of this seat of the national government has produced in me nothing but absolute loathing and disgust."

In one sense, Adams' rise to the presidency was unique in American politics. Like many another American, he wanted badly to be President—and for many reasons:

partly because of his lofty patriotism; partly because it was the greatest honor to which an American could aspire; partly because he wanted to equal his father's record.

At the same time, Adams' uncompromising integrity and his austere reserve ruled out any attempt at stooping for public favor. "Baby-kissing" and all other pretenses of "folksiness" were deeply repugnant to him. If he was to be elected President, it would be on the basis of sheer, proven merit. He was a statesman, not a politician. His backers were in despair.

What made his attitude all the more unrealistic was that his rivals were flamboyant personalities, skilled in the arts of political manipulation. Not that Adams was blind to the realities of the situation. In 1819, five years before the presidential contest, he declared: "There is not in either house of Congress an individual member who would open his lips to defend me or move a finger to defeat any combination to injure me." And yet he proudly insisted that if "my country wants my services, she must ask for them."

In those days there were no nominating conventions. There were four candidates for President—all from the Republican Party. Campaign activities were limited to newspaper articles and editorials. In some states, the presidential electors were chosen by popular vote; in other states, the electors were chosen by the legislature.

In the election of 1824, Andrew Jackson, the hero of the Battle of New Orleans, had the largest number of votes, with Adams second. But, as Jackson lacked a majority, the election was thrown into the House of

Representatives. Henry Clay, who hated Jackson, threw the votes of his supporters to Adams. Thus Adams became President, even though he had originally received only a third of the votes of the presidential electors.

The new President was not popular. During the campaign he had sadly recorded his realization that "my cause is the cause of truth and honesty and of my country. There is hardly a bad passion of the human heart but is arrayed against me." And he had added: "I need advice very much and I have no one to advise me."

No other President has ever carried nonpartisanship to such an extreme as John Quincy Adams. In appointing his cabinet he chose men who had not supported him in the campaign. In fact, some of them had done their best to block his path to the presidency. By making his appointments purely on the basis of merit, Adams proved that he was sincere in insisting that ability should be the only basis for political appointment.

Later, when many of his appointees intrigued against him while they were in office, he refused to discharge them. Doubtless he was furious at their treachery, but stern devotion to his statesmanlike principles outweighed his anger.

During the four years of his term, he discharged only twelve officeholders—in each case for perfectly valid reasons. When Adams was asked to remove a government official whose attacks on him were creating a public scandal, he replied in words that have been heard from no other American President:

"Should I remove this man for this cause, it must be

upon some fixed principle, which would apply to others as well as to him. And where was it possible to draw the line? Of the custom house officers throughout the Union four-fifths, in all probability, were opposed to my election. They were all now in my power, and I had been urged very earnestly to sweep away my opponents and provide, with my places, for my friends."

This was of course the very policy that was followed a few years later by Andrew Jackson when he became President. But Adams despised the notorious policy of "To the victor belong the spoils." He continued his explanation:

"I can justify the refusal to adopt this policy only by the steadiness and consistency of my adhesion to my own policy. If I depart from this in one instance, I shall be called on by my friends to do the same thing in many. An insidious and inquisitorial scrutiny into the personal dispositions of public officers will creep through the whole Union, and the most selfish and sordid passions will be kindled into activity to distort the conduct and misrepresent the feelings of men whose places may become the prize of slander upon them."

These are the words of the great American, valid not only for Adams' administration, but for all administrations.

In seeking the presidency, Adams had projected a magnificent program of public improvements. But his defeated rivals, their eyes on the election of 1828, made a point of automatically blocking every proposal. Adams' hands were tied, and he achieved none of his ambitions. His time was spent on the kind of trifles he had described in his diary when he was Secretary of State:

"Members of Congress, visitors at the office, occupied again all the hours of business. Every man comes with a story, demand, or solicitations of his own; almost every one comes to ask favors. No sooner has one left the office than another enters. . . . I have not time to write the name of one who retires before another comes in. Eight or ten thus succeed one another without leaving a moment's interval. When they are gone, often while some of them are here, comes in a mail of letters, dispatches, and newspapers. Pressing business of the office, suspended while the visitors are with me, admits of no further delay. The sun goes down on business uncompleted."

But even this depressing story had its lighter side. Adams was a firm believer in exercise and loved to swim, keeping up this activity even in advanced old age. As Secretary and President, he often went swimming in the Potomac, on one occasion remaining in the water for over an hour.

A visitor who wanted to be sure of getting to see the President arrived one morning before dawn at the banks of the Potomac. Soon he saw "a gentleman, in nankeen pantaloons, and a blue pea jacket, walking rapidly from the White House towards the river. This was John Quincy Adams, President of the United States. I moved off to a respectful distance. The President began to disrobe before he reached a tree on the brink of the river, where he deposited his clothes, and then plunged in head first and then struck out fifteen or twenty rods, swimming rapidly and turning occasionally on his back, seeming as much at ease in that element as upon terra firma. Coming out, he rubbed himself thoroughly with napkins, which he had brought for that purpose in his hand.

The sun had not yet risen when he had dressed himself and was returning to the presidential mansion."

Imagine such a scene in modern times!

That Adams could not be re-elected was a foregone conclusion. His opponents kept up a steady rain of attack on him; the more ridiculous the charges, the more readily they were believed. A favorite theme was that he had been corrupted by the aristocratic courts of Europe, and had nothing in common with the ordinary citizen. For example, when he bought a set of chessmen for the presidential mansion, it was charged that he made this purchase with public funds; and anyway, what red-blooded American played chess?! Adams replied that the purchase had of course been made with his own money, but his replies never caught up with the charges. Today the chessmen may be seen in the Smithsonian Institution, and the republic still stands.

In the election of 1828, Adams went down to landslide defeat. Thoroughly discredited, and now over sixty, his public career was again apparently finished. Nothing was left to him now but to return to his home, prune his trees, muse in his library, reflect on the ingratitude and gullibility of the American electorate, and piously edit his father's papers.

After two unhappy years of enforced retirement, a delegation of Adams' neighbors sounded him out on the possibility of his running for Congress. They approached the testy old man apologetically: after all, it must have been difficult for a former President to humble himself by serving as a mere Congressman. Not at all, he replied. "No person could be degraded by serving the people as a Representative in Congress. Nor, in my opinion, would an ex-President of the United States be degraded by serving as a selectman of his town, if elected thereto by the people."

Nor was there any pretense in the dignified simplicity of his reply. For, on being elected to the House, he recorded his happiness—and his loneliness—in this pathetic entry:

"My election as President was not half so gratifying to my inmost soul. No election or appointment conferred upon me ever gave me so much pleasure. I say this to record my sentiments; but no stranger intermeddleth with my joys and the dearest of my friends have no sympathy with my sensations."

Once Adams entered Congress, he became its ablest and most distinguished member. He was also its most picturesque and most cantankerous member. His constituents were so pleased with him that they re-elected him for every new term until his death seventeen years later. One unusual feature was his punctual and conscientious attendance at every session. No matter how indisposed he might feel, the public business came before everything else, and he never missed a sitting of the House for any reason.

One of his grandsons later described him as "absorbed in work and public life. He seemed to be always writing—as, indeed, he was . . . a very old-looking gentleman, with a bald head and a white fringe of hair—writing—writing, writing—with a perpetual ink-stain on the forefinger and thumb of the right hand."

The old man's idea of resting from work was to do

other work. "His was not a holiday temperament. Always unaccompanied, he used to wander about the ragged, unkempt old place—with its pear and cherry trees, and old-time orchard—hatchet and saw in hand, pruning and watching his seedlings."

The new Congressman took a lively interest in every public issue and had well-considered views on every problem that faced the country. Of all these issues, one overshadowed all the rest. That issue was slavery.

It had been calculated that during the three centuries and more that the Negro slave trade flourished, about 24,000,000 victims were forcibly removed from the Dark Continent to the unspeakable holds of the slave ships; and that of this number, half died on the voyage. No matter to the slave trader; there was plenty of human raw material left.

A man like Adams, whose every thought invoked the Bible and the Declaration of Independence, could not stomach the existence of slavery in his beloved country. The slaves were deprived of the most elementary civil rights, stripped of every human dignity. Condemned to a lifetime of toil, they were beaten and tortured; their family relationships were ruthlessly broken up whenever it suited the master's whim or profit.

Appalled by the plight of these unfortunates, Adams eloquently described them as "cursed by the mere color of their skin, already doomed by their complexion to drudge in the lowest offices of society, excluded by their color from all the refined enjoyments of life accessible to others, excluded from the benefits of a liberal education."

Day after day the unthinking heartlessness of slavery was borne in on the old man. Here is a typical entry, written in 1840:

"Joseph Cartwright, a preacher of a colored Methodist church, came this morning with a subscription book to raise $450 to purchase the freedom of his three grandchildren—two girls and one boy, all under three or four years of age. He told me that he had been upwards of twenty years in purchasing his own freedom and that of his three sons."

Aside from the moral issue, there were other disquieting aspects of slavery. The Constitution provided that when the population of a state was counted for purposes of apportioning its quota of Congressmen, every five Negroes were to be counted as three additional inhabitants. This gave the South some twenty additional Representatives at a time when the membership of the House totaled less than 200. Supreme irony, that the helpless Negro, deprived of every civil right, was utilized to exercise a kind of veto on antislavery and every other kind of liberal legislation in Congress! Thus the continued existence of slavery was inextricably bound up with the defeat of other causes that Adams held dear.

And yet, with his Puritan sternness, Adams for a long time refused to lift his voice against slavery. For the Founding Fathers, those men whom he venerated, had written slavery into the Constitution. A bargain was a bargain, and had to be kept. Yet Adams' policy changed imperceptibly as the years went on: he foresaw the terrible outcome of the heated struggle over the admission of new states as free states or slave states.

Thoughtfully observing the great debate on the Missouri Compromise of 1820, Adams had written in his diary: "Slavery is the great and foul stain upon the North American Union. If the Union must be dissolved, slavery is precisely the question upon which it ought to break. For the present, however, this contest is laid asleep." Somehow, some day, emancipation was bound to come. "A life devoted to it," he noted in his diary, "would be nobly spent or sacrificed."

Once elected to Congress, Adams was embroiled in the struggle over slavery with unforeseen suddenness. One of his first acts as a Congressman was to present a petition to abolish slavery in the District of Columbia. Adams was not in favor of such abolition because slavery was recognized in the Constitution. But the right of petition was guaranteed in the Constitution. To Adams this right was sacred: every Congressman had a duty to present such petitions to Congress even if he disagreed with their contents.

Hardly a single member of Congress shared Adams' strong convictions on this subject. In fact, many of them were deeply hostile; they did not relish the appearance of petitions opposing some favorite interest of their own.

This was particularly true of the members from slave states. They soon developed a technique of "tabling" all resolutions and petitions against slavery: they quietly buried these documents without action or even discussion. This was the infamous "Gag Rule," against which Adams carried on his gallant fight for fourteen years.

Actually there was a whole series of gag rules, each provoked by Adams until, after years of struggle, he had finally fashioned a majority to defeat the slavery forces. This running battle produced the wildest scenes ever seen in Congress, with the Speaker vainly striving to return the agitated House to its customary decorum.

It is difficult to imagine the dreary friendlessness of Adams' position in the early years of this long struggle. The slaveowners hated Adams because he was a menace. Northern businessmen had no use for him because they wanted no change in their highly profitable business relations with the South. Even the abolitionists looked down on him because of differences of opinion with him.

Calhoun, the leader of the Southern bloc, was expressing himself with studied mildness when he called Adams "a mischievous, bad old man." Those who sympathized with Adams nevertheless were too faint-hearted to come openly to his side and share the brunt of the battle.

It was easy to dismiss Adams as a senile crank, a willful exhibitionist, a provocative troublemaker. His conscience would not allow him to look on unprotestingly at the triumph of injustice. But he had a practical purpose as well: by means of his controversies he was educating his fellow citizens and awakening them to the existence of momentous issues which they would have preferred to ignore. They could not remain unimpressed by his courageous fight when they read such sweeping resolutions as this one, specifically passed to silence Adams:

"Resolved, That all petitions, memorials, resolutions,

propositions, or papers, relating in any way, or to any extent whatever, to the subject of slavery, shall, without being either printed or referred, be laid upon the table, and that no further action whatever shall be had thereon."

Who could say where such sweeping repression would end, or to what other areas it would spread? Adams not only fought the Gag Rule; with characteristic daring, he even counterattacked. In one of his many debates, he lashed back at his Southern opponents with the claim that "when a country is invaded, and two hostile armies are set in martial array, the commanders of both armies have power to emancipate all the slaves in the invaded territory."

When Adams stated majestically that "I lay this down as the law of the nations," he had behind him all the prestige of his many distinguished years in the diplomatic service. His knowledge of international law was second to none. When he claimed that the President of the United States had power to free the slaves *in wartime,* his words left an unforgettable impression. Twenty years later, at the height of the Civil War, President Abraham Lincoln applied the Adams doctrine when he issued the Emancipation Proclamation to free the slaves in the states that had seceded from the Union.

If Adams was troubled by his friendless state, he confined his despair to his diary. There was no limit to his sarcasm, no dearth of parliamentary tricks that always caught his opponents off balance. He answered insult with insult; ridicule he turned back with even more withering contempt.

A reporter watching Adams from the press gallery described him in these words:

"Alone, unspoken to, unconsulted, never consulting with others, he sits apart, wrapped in his reveries. . . . He looks enfeebled, but yet he is never tired; worn out, but ever ready for unending combat; melancholy, but let a witty thing fall from any member and that old man's face is wreathed in smiles."

The slavery issue was by no means the only one on which Adams lavished his devotion. A wealthy Englishman named James Smithson willed a considerable sum of money to the people of the United States "for the increase and diffusion of knowledge among men." Most members of Congress were either indifferent or downright hostile. Some were interested—to the extent of planning how the money could be squandered by creating useless jobs for political hacks.

Adams alone had the vision to realize what could be done with the legacy. Eloquently and stubbornly the old man fought for the establishment of a museum. He arranged for a congressional committee to handle the bequest and was appointed chairman. It took years of constant effort by Adams to establish the Smithsonian Institution in the nation's capital—and during most of the time he was involved in the struggle over slavery. Thus we owe this magnificent museum to Adams' unceasing efforts to bring it into existence.

The endless hours of wrangling in Congress were not the only drain on the old man's energies. As he had no secretary, he had to spend many additional hours writing with his trembling hand, copying each petition, composing speeches, answering correspondents, recording the battles in his diary. Toilsome days of wearisome argument alternated with agitated, sleepless nights.

The strain was intensified by the frequent threats of assassination he received. For example: "I shall be in Washington next March and I shall shoot you. *Remember!!!*" Another read: "On the first day of May next I promise to cut your throat from ear to Ear." While Adams ignored these threats, they nevertheless depressed him; for they proved, if proof were needed, that slavery degrades the master as well as the slave.

At the opening of the 1836 session, the Southern Congressmen played their trump card. When Adams tried to present a petition of nine ladies of Fredericksburg, Virginia, on the subject of slavery, a South Carolina Congressman introduced this resolution:

"Resolved, That the Honorable John Quincy Adams by the attempt just made to introduce a petition purporting on its face to be from slaves, has been guilty of a gross disrespect to this House, and that he be instantly brought to the bar to receive the severe censure of the Speaker."

The object of this maneuver was to censure Adams so brutally that the sensitive, proud old man would resign in disgrace from the House. Yet "Old Man Eloquent" hurled back the attack brilliantly. First he embarrassed his Southern enemies by pointing out that the Fredericksburg ladies actually opposed abolition!

Then he turned to the broad question of petition.

It was, he said, "supplication—it is entreaty—it is prayer." Scornfully he asked his tormentors: "And what does your law say? Does it say that, before presenting a petition, you shall look into it, and see whether it comes from the virtuous, and the great, and the mighty? No, sir, it says no such thing; the right of petition belongs to all."

In the face of this powerful counterattack, the resolution of censure was reworded to criticize Adams for baiting the Southerners and giving them a false impression of the petition. Some peace-loving members of the House moved to table the resolution of censure, but Adams disdainfully brushed the gesture aside. He insisted that the resolution be brought to a vote! Manfully he stuck to his position that petition was a right given by God—"a right to implore a favor, to seek for mercy."

Threatened with being brought before a South Carolina grand jury, the heroic old man stood his ground. "I thank God I am not a citizen of South Carolina! Such a threat when brought before the world, would excite nothing but contempt and amazement." And he concluded in the grand manner: "If the gentleman from South Carolina, by bringing forward the resolution of censure, thinks to frighten me from my purpose, he has mistaken his man. I am not to be intimidated by him, nor by all the Grand Juries of the Universe."

Frankly admitting that censure by the House would be the heaviest calamity of his life, he nevertheless refused to budge an inch: "Not a single word of what I have said do I unsay; nay, I am ready to do and say the same tomorrow."

And, although the vast majority of the House was against him, the resolution of censure was defeated by a resounding vote of 137 to 21! Even Adams' enemies were so impressed by his courage and eloquence that many of them voted in his favor. This reluctant support was the greatest personal tribute ever offered to John Quincy Adams.

The years passed, and at the beginning of every session the old man put the House into a wild uproar by defying the Gag Rule as he attempted to read petitions against slavery.

Finally his baffled enemies thought up a new way to badger him. They sent him a petition asking that all free Negroes be deported or sold into slavery. Abhorrent as the petition was to Adams, he remained true to his principles and presented the petition to Congress.

Next they sent him a petition requesting that he be tried by the House as a public enemy. Adams presented the petition.

Another petition called for Adams' dismissal from the chairmanship of the Committee on Foreign Affairs on the claim that he was crazy. Calmly Adams presented the petition.

At last his enemies sent him a petition asking that the Union be dissolved. And, though the Union was dearer to Adams than anything else in the world, he presented the petition.

At last—so it seemed—he had been maneuvered into a trap from which there was no escape. In 1842 a new resolution of censure was introduced because he had presented a petition calling for the breakup of the Union.

Adams had foreseen this threat of disaster. A year earlier he had written in his diary: "The world, the flesh, and all the devils in hell are arrayed against any men who now in this North American Union shall dare to join the standard of Almighty God to put down the African slave-trade; and what can I, upon the verge of my seventy-fourth birthday, with a shaking hand, a darkening eye, a drowsy brain, and with all my faculties dropping one by one, as the teeth are dropping from my head—what can I do for the cause of God and man?" But, still heedful of the lessons taught him in childhood by John and Abigail Adams, he had added: "Yet my conscience presses me on."

And so, despite his advanced age and infirmities, "Old Man Eloquent" fought back fiercely. He called upon the Clerk of the House to read the noble opening sentences of the Declaration of Independence. A feeling of awe descended on the House as Adams pointed out that the Declaration asserted "the right of the people to alter, to change, to destroy, the Government if it becomes oppressive to them."

Adams went on to ridicule his enemies for their impudence in accusing him of high treason. Only the Constitution could determine the nature of treason. The debate went on for two weeks and was marked by the grossest personal abuse of the old man. In the course of these attacks, his enemies bluntly ranked him with Benedict Arnold and Aaron Burr.

Once more Adams fought back dauntlessly. "I am still in the power of the majority," he proclaimed. "If they say they will try me, they must try me. If they say they will punish me, they must punish me. If they say that, in grace and mercy, they will spare me, I disdain and cast their mercy away; and I ask them if they will come to such a trial and expel me. I defy them."

This time the motion to censure Adams was defeated by a vote of 106 to 93. This was the high point of the attempt of the slavery forces to gag Adams. The opposition to slavery had increased to such an extent in the North that Adams now had considerable popular backing for his struggle against the Gag Rule. On December 3, 1844, when Adams was seventy-seven years old, he had the delicious satisfaction of commanding a majority (108 to 80) for the first time. It was the end of the Gag Rule. Immediately he rubbed salt into his opponents' wounds by offering almost two hundred petitions in succession! Thus ended the old man's grueling, lonely struggle to preserve for the American people one of its most precious rights.

Five years earlier, Adams had celebrated a great personal triumph against slavery. This was in the famous *Amistad* case, which came about in this way:

Some African Negroes had been illegally smuggled into Cuba. From there they had been taken on the *Amistad* by Spanish slavers who intended to dispose of them illegally on American soil. The Negroes had revolted, killed the officers, and ordered the crew to sail for Africa. A short time later the ship was seized by an American navy cutter.

The slavers brought suit in an American court to have the Negroes turned over to them. The Negroes, on the other hand, rightly claimed that they were entitled to their freedom since they had been seized illegally and had acted in self-defense. The case aroused enormous interest; Adams, because of his distinguished public position, was asked to plead the cause of the Negroes before the Supreme Court.

At first the old man was afraid to take the case, because of his enfeebled state; but in the end he allowed himself to be persuaded. "I implore the mercy of Almighty God," he prayed, "so as to control my temper, to enlighten my soul, and to give me utterance, that I may prove myself in every respect equal to the task." Still fearing that he might ruin the case, he wrote in his diary, "O, how shall I do justice to the case and to these men?"

But his doubts only spurred him to prepare his defense with great skill and care. When the old man rose to face the justices of the Supreme Court, all his fears were forgotten. He spoke that day for four and a half hours, and took three hours the next day to complete his analysis of the case. Throughout that time he held the absorbed attention of the judges and the spectators. With all the pressures of the government lined up against him, Adams' powerful arguments won over the justices. The Negroes were freed.

When Adams went on a family sight-seeing trip four years later, he discovered to his great surprise that he had become a popular man. Wherever his train stopped, he was amazed at the huge crowds and stormy ovations. At the town of Batavia, New York, there was such a crush of people who wanted to shake hands with him that the platform collapsed. Characteristically, these demonstrations left Adams "shamefaced and awkward"—yet grateful. He had mellowed after all, and shook hands readily with his admirers.

Later he went on to Akron and Cincinnati, where he was applauded by equally enthusiastic crowds. So popular was he that pretty young women pushed and shoved for the privilege of kissing him.

One morning in 1846, when Adams was seventy-nine years old and still getting up before dawn, he suffered a paralytic stroke. He recovered in a few days but never fully regained his strength. On his first appearance in Congress in 1847, the feeble old man received a standing ovation from all the members. Deeply moved, he thanked them in a low, trembling voice.

On February 21, 1848, during a session of the House, Adams had a second stroke. He lingered on for two more days, and shortly before he died, he murmured, "This is the last of earth, I am content."

Scores of memorial meetings were held in honor of "Old Man Eloquent." No monuments were erected to him, but to this day visitors to the House are shown the unpretentious bronze marker which was placed at the spot where he fell.

All his life Adams held strong convictions which he had arrived at by independent thinking. Nothing was further from his mind than the shabby compromises that men in politics often resort to in order to further their careers. He never hesitated to express his convictions, no matter what the cost might be in terms of his career.

People complained of his cold manner, yet he could be deeply affectionate. He had no abundance of small talk, yet he could hold the attention of huge audiences with speeches several hours long. Though he never toadied for approval, he nevertheless remained in office for over half a century, with only very slight gaps.

Adams had qualities which appealed to the Americans of his day. He was scrupulously honest in all his dealings. His deep, glowing patriotism was always his guide in every action he took. As one of the last remaining links with the Founding Fathers, he was regarded with awe.

Adams' readiness to express his convictions and fight for them against overwhelming odds secured for him the sympathy that always goes to the underdog. Even his enemies admired his fighting qualities and on several remarkable occasions paid him reluctant tributes despite themselves. All the world respects a grand fighter, and few men have been as rugged, as forthright, and as unselfishly patriotic as John Quincy Adams.

HORACE MANN

Be ashamed to die until you have won some victory for humanity.

In the United States, 1837 was a year of "fear, greed, confusion, unemployment, misery, distress." Rich and poor alike felt the effects of the most far-reaching financial panic that had ever gripped the country.

The feverish sale and resale of western lands had pyramided their prices to a level that had no realistic relation to their true value. "Wild-cat" banks foolishly overextended themselves by making loans to speculators. When the bubble burst, land values plunged disastrously. Land that had been selling for twenty-five dollars an acre went down to five dollars an acre.

In a short time, half the real property in the country changed hands in distress sales. Banks, unable to meet their obligations or cover their deposits, had to close their doors. In a few months there were 33,000 business failures in New York City alone—losses involving millions of dollars. In the South, slaveowners dumped their slaves on the market because it was too expensive to feed them. The cities were plague spots of unemployment and suffering. In Washington, the Federal administration looked on helplessly: in those days, economic distress was a disaster that had to be allowed to run its course.

It was in this grim year that the newly formed Massachusetts Board of Education started its work. State legislatures were in no mood to "squander" money on education. This was the atmosphere in which Horace Mann began his heroic work as Secretary of the state board.

Mann came naturally enough by his love of learning and his interest in education. Both of his parents, as well as several relatives, had been teachers. His sister Rebecca, according to a Massachusetts governor, was "the best teacher in the world." To the Mann family, a book was something indescribably precious; merely to hold a volume in one's hand was a source of pleasure.

Horace Mann's ancestors came to New England during the early waves of Puritan migration in the seventeenth century, when thousands of Puritans left their homeland to escape religious persecution. The little town in which Horace Mann was born had been settled in 1660. More than a century later, after receiving a gift of books from Benjamin Franklin, its citizens had gratefully renamed their town after that unpretentious philosopher, statesman, and jack of so many other trades.

Horace was born in 1796, the fourth child in his family. His boyhood was harsh, devoted to working from sunup to sundown on his father's farm. Years later, looking back to those early days, he could no longer remember when he had started to work. "Even my play-hours—not play-days for I never had any, but my play-hours—were earned by extra exertion, finishing tasks early to gain a little leisure for boyish sports."

When Horace was thirteen, his father died and the family found itself in desperate circumstances. The boy continued to work on the farm and also helped his mother to braid straw for a hat factory. It was a hard life, and yet "all my boyish castles in the air," he recalled many years later, "had reference to doing something for the benefit of mankind."

Sunday morning and afternoon were given up to long church services, with sermons that hammered away at such gruesome themes as, "Learn the duty of mourners which is unconditioned submission—God has taken his pleasure and they know not what it is. . . . If mankind know so little about death before it comes, then it is not strange that it should be the king of terrors."

Such talk was not congenial to a boy of Horace Mann's darting, imaginative, impatient spirit. Until he was sixteen, his schooling was limited to ten weeks a year. To some extent he escaped from his cramped surroundings by devouring every one of the history books in the town's tiny library. He avoided the forty volumes of sermons.

From time to time Horace was absent from church to go swimming—another dreadful act of rebellion. On one of these occasions his older brother was drowned. To the minister's way of thinking, this was divine punishment, and he preached a bitter, unrelenting sermon about "the lake which burneth with fire and brimstone." For years Horace was to be plagued by nightmares of "a bottomless and seething lake, filled with torments," and he heard the wailings of the victims in his sleep.

Horace knew that the life of a farmer was not for him. He wanted to be a lawyer. When he was nineteen he began studying Greek, Latin, and mathematics with teachers who wandered from town to town. In this way he learned enough to be able to enter Brown University in 1816. The tuition charge in those days amounted to twenty dollars a term.

Though fresh from the farm, the young man proved to be the most brilliant student of his time at Brown. He was also the most popular student, for he made friends easily and he had the knack of being witty without being malicious. His classmates felt that he had the makings of a great lawyer; a few realized that he was versatile enough to achieve fame in more than one field.

His favorite college course was oratory, and before his student days were over he had become an exceptionally skillful debater. At the class graduation in 1819

Mann received the highest honor—orator at the Examination Dinner of his class. In a prophetic phrase he compared education to Jacob's Ladder—it should "reach from earth to heaven."

After graduation, Mann, like most young lawyers, spent several trying years getting established in his profession. At first his progress was discouragingly slow, and cases were few and far between. But gradually he made a name for himself, for he left a lasting impression wherever he went. He knew how to prepare a case and he was a formidable opponent in the courtroom. But he had other assets as well—his attractive personality and his unmistakable integrity quickly inspired confidence and trust.

Lucrative but shabby cases held no interest for him: "Never espouse the wrong side of a cause knowingly," he later advised young lawyers; "and if, unwittingly, you find yourself on the wrong side, leap out of it as quick as you would jump out of a vat of boiling brimstone, should you accidentally fall into one."

In 1827, when Mann was only thirty-one, he was elected to the Massachusetts Legislature. Three years later he married Charlotte Meser, a daughter of the President of Brown University. It was a real love match, and when his wife died only two years later, Mann was dazed and helpless. The ensuing years of a dreary widower's life in a boardinghouse only deepened his tendency to brooding melancholy.

In the circumstances it was natural for Mann to plunge into his legislative work with greater vigor than ever. "Hopeless" causes attracted him—partly because they called for a fight against great odds, partly because he needed some outlet for the tenderness and devotion which could no longer be lavished on his wife.

Mann was fortunate in living in an age of reform—and indeed there were many dreadful conditions that called for drastic change. The treatment of insane people, for example, had made virtually no progress since the Middle Ages. There was little scientific understanding of these unfortunates, and even less sympathy for them. They were penned up in filthy jails, clothed in rags, fed on slops, and often kept in chains. Here and there a few unusual people, gifted with insight and compassion, realized that there was much to be learned about treating the insane and possibly curing them.

In Mann's time the general approach to this problem was still to shunt the insane aside and prevent them from doing any harm; the idea of treating them kindly or trying to cure them was a freakish notion that pained the taxpayer and aroused contempt or ridicule among the general public.

Despite this widespread attitude, Mann put through a successful fight in the Legislature to establish the first state insane asylum. He had become interested in this problem because throughout his life he always tried to improve community services, despite the stubborn opposition of people who were set in the old ways and who begrudged whatever expense was involved. In this case, Mann had been inspired to fight for a modern Massachusetts asylum by the recent construction of a new Connecticut hospital to provide better treatment.

By appealing to the local pride of Governor Lincoln, Mann obtained the powerful backing he needed for the project. For the first time inmates were given pleasant surroundings and considerate treatment. In this struggle Mann was revealed as a persuasive advocate and a relentless debater who was not afraid of fighting against seemingly overwhelming odds.

Mann now turned to another problem—imprisonment for debt, which in those days was one of the most inhumane features of American law. Peter Cooper, writing his autobiography in the 1870's, recalled the time when "unmarried white men could be sold for debt in the state of Connecticut."

Some of the cases were harrowing beyond belief. In one instance, a blind man with a family to support was imprisoned for a debt of six dollars. A Providence widow was jailed for a debt of sixty-eight cents! And, to make this tragedy even more fantastic, it was found that her husband had lost his life while attempting to guard the creditor's property. In Salem, a Bunker Hill veteran seventy-six years old was jailed for a debt of a few dollars.

It has been estimated that in 1828, at least 75,000 Americans were imprisoned for being unable to pay their debts. In more than half of the cases, the amount involved was less than twenty dollars; and, of course, while the victims were in prison there was no way for them to clear the debt. In Boston alone, 1300 men and 100 women were in prison for debt.

To change this pattern was not easy: the substantial citizens of every community felt that people would pay their debts only if the threat of imprisonment were held over their heads, and that to remove this threat would weaken the moral fiber of the American nation.

But Mann, well aware of the discontent among farmers and workingmen, joined the fight against debt imprisonment. Although it took years to repeal the debt laws in their entirety, the reformers managed to make step-by-step progress in doing away with the harsh penalties.

These successes were gratifying; but Mann was too restless, and too dissatisfied with the world as he found it, to be content with what he had accomplished thus far. His was not the kind of temperament that can accept the spineless concept of "Whatever is, is right." All his life he was to be driven by the ideal of making the world a better place to live in, of enriching and ennobling the lives of his fellow human beings.

Because education, as we shall see, seemed to Mann the most important of all human activities, he made a thoroughgoing study of the school systems of his time. These systems were bad—bad in almost every respect. Anyone else would have been so filled with disgust and hopelessness that he would have turned away in despair. Others had tried their hand at improving the schools, and of course Mann benefited by their insights. But none of his forerunners had his vision, persuasiveness, organizing powers, or his flair for enlisting prominent citizens in the struggle. Mann's reaction was characteristically different: once he had a clear-eyed picture of the evils, he determined to devote the rest of his life to improving the Massachusetts school system.

His own schooldays had been among the dreariest of his life. Since then, conditions had worsened. For one thing, attendance was a hit-or-miss affair. Poverty was so pervasive that parents readily handed over their children to the drudgery of the new textile mills. We get some idea of what the conditions must have been when we read that it was considered a great step forward when Massachusetts passed a law in 1842 limiting the work day of children *under twelve* to only ten hours a day.

Schools were cramped, uncomfortable, and cheerless. The monotony of learning was not relieved by maps or charts or flowers or blackboards in a single classroom. Discipline was of the "good, old-fashioned" variety. In a typical Boston school of 400 pupils there was an average of sixty-five whippings daily.

A report on the Massachusetts schools spoke in scathing terms of "the nakedness and deformity of the schools, the comfortless and dilapidated buildings, the unhung doors, broken sashes, absent panes, yawning roofs, and muddy, moldering floors."

Equally unsparing was the report's criticism of the teachers, who for the most part were "low, vulgar, obscene, intemperate, and utterly incompetent to teach anything good." And no wonder—for the teachers received no professional training and were paid wretchedly low salaries.

A painstaking study of all the schools revealed that only a third were in good repair; another third were reasonably comfortable; the rest were "unfit for man or beast." About half the schools had no playground; almost as many lacked convenient seats and desks. Similarly, a large number had virtually no ventilation and no toilet facilities.

Any chance for improvement was crippled by the system of supporting schools from local property taxes. These were paid by the well-to-do members of the community, who sent their own children to private schools. Thus they had no personal interest in improving the public schools; in fact, then as now, their only goal was lower taxes, which in turn meant lower standards for schools. In this atmosphere Mann's clear call for "universal, free, tax-supported, public" education inevitably stirred up ferocious indignation.

Since property qualifications for voting still existed in many states, the very people who would be most likely to want a better public educational system were debarred from voting. The ballot was limited to the very people who were most strongly opposed to spending money to improve the schools. In Rhode Island, for example, the voting qualifications were so unreasonable that in this state of 108,000 people, 1800 strategically distributed votes were enough to control the election of the whole state legislature.

In 1837 Massachusetts finally started the long-needed overhaul of its school system. The Legislature set up a statewide Board of Education which was to establish uniform standards, raise the level of teaching, secure better textbooks, put the schools on a sounder financial basis, and do away with the evils of the old system.

But everything depended on the selection of the Secretary, on whose shoulders the hard work would fall. If the Secretary was mediocre, or indifferent, or a political hack, things would move along in the same old rut. If he was a brilliant, dedicated man, devoted to steady improvement and the introduction of new ideas; if he was willing to work eighteen hours a day for a pitifully inadequate salary; if he had the determination and persuasiveness to overcome the hostility of the taxpayers and the indifference of the legislators, then there was a bare chance that some good might be accomplished.

So the whole fate of the law, and of the Massachusetts school system, narrowed down to the selection of the Secretary. Even more than the fate of one state system was involved; the cause of education in the United States as a whole was at stake. For the Massachusetts state board was the first of its kind. If it succeeded, other states would follow suit. If the experiment failed, then educational progress in the United States would receive a stunning blow.

Who then would be the new Secretary? The handful of distinguished people who understood the issue wanted Horace Mann to become the first Secretary. As President of the Massachusetts State Senate since 1836, he had played a leading role in the struggle to get the new law passed. But he had built up a lucrative law practice in Dedham, and he had brilliant political prospects. With his popularity and recognized ability, the state governorship and a seat in the United States

Senate were sure to be his in a few years. Was he t
sacrifice such glittering distinctions for a post in which
he would have feeble support against continual opposition, while at the same time he labored under the
handicap of a greatly reduced income?

Horace Mann accepted the appointment. He was
passionately absorbed in the improvement of the public
schools, and he knew how vitally important this is in
a democracy. Now at last he had the chance to put
his principles into practice. He had no illusions about
the difficulties of the job, and about the obstacles and
frustrations that it would bring. But he would have been
untrue to himself if he had made the obvious calculation
and turned down the opportunity to serve.

Before we see what Horace Mann accomplished for
education, it will be useful to have some idea of his
appearance, his character, and the impression he made
on other people.

Mann had a striking appearance and a radiant personality. He was slender, erect, and over six feet tall.
He had sparkling eyes and an attractively resonant
voice. His hair turned gray while he was still fairly
young. In later years a reporter described him as a
"tall, straight, thin gentleman with white hair, gold-
rimmed spectacles, black clothes, and firm, quick mo-
tions."

Mann liked interesting conversation and had a knack
of making any subject absorbing. But he did not mo-
nopolize the conversation; he knew how to draw out

so that they rose, so to speak, above
of their usual interests.

ped by shyness as a young man, he
serviceable quality when it came
ople at their ease. His deeply affectionate
and his instinctive kindness were so marked even
to perfect strangers that people who met him for a
few minutes still recalled the occasion with awe fifty
years later. He loved children and they in turn took
to him at once.

Mann was so scrupulous in his dealings with other
people that he often went to a great deal of trouble
to make sure he was not hurting someone's feelings or
wronging him unknowingly.

On the other hand, he was oversensitive to criticism,
possibly because so much of it was unfair and unin-
formed. His ideals were so lofty that he often judged
opponents too harshly. About the things that he felt
deeply, there was no middle region, so far as he was
concerned, between absolute right and absolute wrong.

Few people, perhaps none, could live up to Mann's
high ideals. Much of his occasional severity, it is true,
came from the harried life he led, the constant sequence
of maddening problems. Only a man of great determination could endure such tension, and such a man can
easily overshoot the mark when he is striving to remove a frustrating obstacle from his path.

Mann was an American patriot in the best sense of
the words. He loved his country deeply, and wanted to
contribute whatever he could to make it better and
finer. There was nothing flashy about his patriotism,

and he abhorred the flag-waving speeches of the typical politician.

Mann was one of the great public speakers of his time. He built up his speeches so logically that his audiences were lifted up to his level when he spoke about matters that ordinarily were of no interest to them. He knew how to arouse people, how to make them more reflective, how to appeal to what was noblest in them. Only when a democracy has such leaders can it flourish.

Though Mann never talked down to audiences, he applied wit and humor skillfully to hold their interest. Yet these devices were only means to an end—to take people out of the rut of uninspired thinking and purely selfish desires.

All of Mann's educational work was done at the cost of heavy financial sacrifices. His meager salary was rarely paid on time. For years he went without lunch in order to economize. It has been estimated that if he had continued his law career his income would have been five times greater; it certainly would have been less precarious.

Some of Mann's difficulties were eased when he married his second wife, Mary Peabody, in 1843, eleven years after the death of his first wife. This highly intelligent and well-educated woman helped her husband immeasurably as a skilled translator and secretary. In this way she kept Mann abreast of educational reforms and innovations in England, France, Germany, and Switzerland and helped him with his correspondence. But what was even more important, she was an affectionate wife and tender mother who made his home a refuge from the tensions and struggles of his work for the public schools. Thanks to her, his occasional asperity was softened as his effectiveness was increased.

As we have seen, it must have cost Mann quite a pang to renounce his brilliant prospects as a lawyer. He summed up his fateful decision in a single sentence that was a winning blend of nobility, humor, and resignation. "Let the next generation be my client," he said.

To prepare himself for his new task as Secretary, Mann made an exhaustive study of current educational theories. He began a painstaking census of the number of schoolchildren and teachers. He traveled from town to town, tirelessly preaching the gospel of public-school education. He sought every opportunity to discuss his ideas with outstanding teachers.

Wherever he went he was cheerful, resourceful, full of infectious enthusiasm for the schools. No one could guess that his diary was strewn with entries like this one: "To make an impression in Berkshire in regard to the public schools is like attempting to batter down Gibraltar with one's fist."

The lack of public libraries also troubled Mann. In 1838 some three hundred libraries were maintained by private subscription in Massachusetts. Against this, there were at most fifteen public libraries in the whole state. Few people worried about the lack of public libraries, fewer still wanted to do something about it.

But to wring his hands and look on helplessly was not Mann's way. To remedy the situation, he arranged for a standard set of books to be published by the state to stock school libraries supported by each town. This minimum collection would form a basis for further expansion. Despite strong opposition from reluctant taxpayers and religious fanatics, Mann had his way. Later on, though, this temporary success was to involve Mann in one of his most dangerous controversies.

Another project dear to Mann's heart was the founding of "normal schools" to train teachers for their work. Previously anyone could become a teacher without any professional training whatever. Here again Mann trod on some sensitive toes; but, despite the fierce opposition that now appeared automatically on the part of people who opposed new ideas and new taxes, he was able to open the first normal school in 1839.

The school started with thirty students, many of them weak in such subjects as grammar and arithmetic. Cyrus Pierce, Mann's good friend and one of the great teachers of the age, grimly described his pupils as "all sorts of odds and ends."

To have to start the program with such mediocre pupils was depressing. To have to begin with a sizable deficit because of the Legislature's budget-paring was even more depressing. Though Mann was far from wealthy, he paid half the deficit out of his own pocket. In addition he sold his law library and donated the proceeds to provide comfortable furniture and other amenities for the students' boardinghouse.

With such sacrifices Mann made it possible for the school to function successfully. Soon he planned three more state schools for teachers. Once more he toured the state, making speech after speech to line up support for the new project. Eventually these pioneering teacher-training schools established by Horace Mann were to be copied throughout the United States.

For ten years he wrote articles for the *Common School Journal* (founded by him for the discussion of school problems) without taking a penny for pay. In these articles we find an unusual combination of generous idealism and shrewd practical sense. Here is a typical passage from one of his articles about the children of poor laborers:

"They were too young to be employed; they were not recognized by local authorities as having any right to the privileges of the public school . . . and there, in the midst of Christian people, no more public care was taken for their instruction, than for that of young foxes in the neighboring mountains."

No one could read this sentence with an untroubled conscience. Having established this claim on the reader, Mann went on to show what a huge debt society owed to the parents of these children. For everyone owes "a vast economical debt to that class of people, whose labor has been mainly instrumental in rearing the great material structures of which we so often boast."

Mann went on to remind his readers—and they needed the reminder!—that these laborers "had materially changed the surface of the earth for our profit and delight, building piers and wharves for our commerce, turning the bed of ocean into dry land for the enlargement of our cities, cutting down the mountains and upheaving the valleys, to smooth the pathway by which distant and alien people might hold communion with one another."

What is remarkable here is that in the grandeur of this eloquent passage Mann was expressing thoughts that had never occurred to his well-to-do readers—nor to the workingmen themselves. He endowed the laborers with a dignity of which they themselves were unconscious.

Having thus made his point effectively, Mann now appealed to the taxpayer's sense of fair play and his self-interest as well:

"Were all considerations of social and Christian duty out of the question, an equitable and fair-minded man ought to blush to receive such benefits without any other requital than just enough food and clothing for the laborers. It is impossible for us to pay them in kind; but there is a compensation which we have the ability to bestow."

And so Mann brings the discussion back to his favorite theme of free, universal, public education:

"We can confer the blessing of education upon their children. And the impulse of duty to do so may lawfully derive additional energy from the reflection that every wise, humane measure adopted for their welfare, directly promotes our own security. For it must be manifest to every forecasting mind, that the children of this people will soon possess the rights of men, whether they possess the *characters* of men or not." (Italics added.)

In 1839 Mann was confronted with unexpected difficulties: a new governor was elected who was completely hostile to public schools. "Economy" was Governor Marcus Morton's watchword. To his way of thinking, public schools were an extravagance.

The Governor's appeal to voters was cynically double-barreled. To the well-off taxpayer he held out the hope of lower taxes by the destruction of the school system; to the poor he held out the hope of "freeing" their children for long hours of work that would add to the family income. This frontal attack was dangerous, for public-school attendance was not yet compulsory. Morton wanted also to close the normal schools and abolish the Board of Education. This would have been a crippling blow.

The Governor had the officeholders, the influential people, and a large section of public opinion on his side. Considering these odds, Mann could hardly have been blamed if he had faltered. But, deeply discouraged though he was, he was one of those rare people who only become more determined in the face of growing danger.

Soon a new menace appeared. A disgruntled author whose books had been refused for the Common School Library widely circulated anonymous letters to the effect that Mann and the Board of Education had plotted to turn all the schoolchildren into Unitarians! The fact was that Mann, while deeply religious, strongly felt that books used in the public schools should be free of any sectarian tinge. Nevertheless, the widely unfair charges alarmed all the sects of Protestant churchgoers as well as the Irish immigrants. The state Legislature's Committee on Education added to the turmoil by issuing

a report calling for the immediate removal of the state
Board of Education. Mann's enemies were closing in for
the kill.

How could one man hold out against such an on-
slaught? During this period Mann's mother died, and
in a moment of depression he wrote in his diary:
"Have not done a particle of work. Thoughts of
homelessness, uselessness, friendlessness—the very ele-
ments out of which suicide is born, press on me with
almost overwhelming intensity." And no wonder! For
Mann, at considerable personal cost, was trying to confer a great blessing on his fellow Americans—the blessing of universal education. Not only did they spurn his
gift and his sacrifice—they turned on him with out-
rageous lies and trumped-up charges.

Yet he had no thought of surrendering. Some of the
most distinguished citizens of the state approved his
work, and he rallied them to save the public-school
system by personally interviewing the legislators with
whom they were acquainted. Their intervention was
effective, for when the destructive committee report
was debated in the Legislature, it was defeated by a vote
of 245 to 182. It was a happy ending in more ways than
one, for he gained new friends for his cause, and even
some enemies of the public schools came over to his side.
Mann had won a great victory, but it was only a battle,
not a war. The struggle would go on.

In 1843 Mann sailed to Europe for his honeymoon
trip. Mann and his bride remained there for ten months

to make an intensive study of the school systems of England, Scotland, Germany, Holland, and France. On his return he wrote a famous report, still worth reading, in which he summed up the good and bad points of the European schools. During his travels he had been favorably impressed with many European schoolteachers, who took an active interest in the children and tried hard to stimulate their love of learning.

Mann's emphasis on this point brought down a stormy attack by a group of Boston schoolmasters whom he had criticized in his report for flogging their pupils. Once more Mann was embroiled in bitter controversies in the form of articles and pamphlets. Though he came out victorious, the endless arguments filled him with a sense of injustice and made him unduly sensitive to criticism.

The following year (1845) brought him a much pleasanter experience when some of the leading citizens of Massachusetts paid him a handsome tribute by raising a substantial sum of money to found two more normal schools. Thus his report on the European schools, with its emphasis on the need for better schools, had made an impression after all.

So the turbulent years took their course, with their struggles and partial victories and slow, gradual achievements. In 1848 new vistas opened for Mann.

After almost two decades of distinguished service in Congress as a representative from Massachusetts, John Quincy Adams died that year. Among those suggested to replace him was Horace Mann. When the idea was broached to him, he replied half-seriously, "To ask anybody in this district to fill Mr. Adams' place is a good deal like asking a mouse to fill an elephant's skin."

Nevertheless many people realized that Mann was well qualified, and he himself, despite his modest reply, was anxious to serve. He felt that a position of national prominence would help him to promote the cause of general education. He may also have believed that his removal from the Massachusetts scene would make his opponents less pugnacious in fighting causes associated with his name.

And there was still another reason—a very pressing one. Despite the fact that his salary was a small one, Mann had repeatedly contributed from his own pocket to make good the needs of normal schools which could not get along on the state's starvation budget. Discussing his contributions with a friend, he said wryly, "I live by tapping my own veins and sucking my own blood." A Congressman's salary, though it was no great sum, would improve his financial situation appreciably. And so he agreed to run for Congress.

As it turned out, Mann was elected by a handsome majority in a special election, and by April he was in Washington to take up his new duties. On the very day of his arrival, an extraordinary event happened that was to involve Mann in an unforeseen crisis.

A sloop left Washington to proceed down the Potomac and sail north. It had a strange "cargo"—seventy-four Negroes, some freedmen, some slaves, some unfortunates whose status was doubtful. They included Daniel Bell, who had purchased his freedom some time ago, as well as that of his wife and eight children, who had been freed in their dead master's will. But now the heirs were contesting the will, and Bell had little hope that his family would be spared.

News of the flight leaked out, and an armed posse stopped the sloop near the mouth of the Potomac. Captain Drayton (the ship's master) and his crew and passengers were tied up and taken back to the capital. An angry mob gathered, crying for the Captain's lynching. During this disgraceful scene, as the Captain later reported, a "slave-trader, armed with a knife, rushed out and made a pass at me which was very near finding its way through my body."

Captain Drayton was a remarkable man. He was well aware, he observed, that "it was asserted in the Declaration of Independence, that all men are born free and equal." And, he added, he "had read in the Bible that God made of one flesh all nations of the earth." Accepting these words in good faith, he felt it his duty to bring the Negroes to freedom. But this was dangerous doctrine in the slave states—and not only in the slave states— when it was applied to Negroes.

Ugly passions ran high in the city; mobs gathered near the jail; furious debates broke out in both houses of Congress. Despite his sympathy for the Negroes, Mann could not make up his mind to help them. When Massachusetts abolitionists begged him to take on the legal defense of the Negroes, he wrote back hesitantly, "I have been so long a stranger to the courts and should be so dull where sharpness is required, that I should probably be about the worst counsel the poor fellows could have."

Yet, despite his doubts, Mann took the case, which like the *Amistad* case defended by John Quincy Adams a few years earlier, had raised public excitement to a high pitch. Mann prudently selected J. M. Carlisle as associate counsel; Carlisle was well versed in Maryland law, which had jurisdiction over the case. The charge against Drayton was that he had carried off the Negroes to sell them in the West Indies. For this act the penalty was death, according to a Maryland statute of 1737. No less than 115 indictments were drawn against Drayton and his two officers.

The courtroom was filled with members of the posse, who brought their weapons. During the trial some of them sat next to Mann and amused themselves by cocking their pistols in order to scare him.

But, despite this menacing atmosphere and the judge's hostile attitude, Mann was not scared. He conducted the defense skillfully, showing inconsistencies in the indictments and glaring contradictions in the testimony. He also pointed out that the death penalty had been abolished in Maryland by a later statute.

In the end, one of Drayton's officers was freed. But Drayton and the remaining officer were found "guilty." Drayton was sentenced to a fine of $10,000 and he was to remain in jail until the fine was paid! Because the abolitionists and their sympathizers had used up their funds to purchase the freedom of as many of the Negroes as they could, they had no money left to pay Drayton's fine.

Drayton's only hope of freedom lay in a presidential pardon. But President Polk, a Southerner, took no action on Drayton's behalf. His successor, Zachary Taylor, was also a Southerner, and he likewise sat by with folded hands. So Drayton remained in prison for four years, until Millard Fillmore became President after Taylor died in office. Fillmore, who hailed from New York, issued a presidential pardon to Drayton.

As for Mann, he never received a penny for his work on the case. Worse yet, it brought him a whole series of misfortunes. He was out of pocket for the expenses he had incurred. He lost many days' salary, as Congressmen were paid in those days on the basis of daily attendance. Finally, he lost part of his pay as Secretary of the Massachusetts Board of Education because of the working time he had lost.

In addition, he was now a marked man as far as the slavery issue was concerned. From this point on, his educational projects would be opposed by all who disagreed with him on this burning issue.

Some years earlier, when Mann was making a speech against slavery, a member of the audience asked him the following question, with the triumphant air of one who is posing a dilemma that admits of no solution: "Would you advance the slaves to an equal social and political condition with the white race?"

This was Mann's reply: "I would give to *every human being* the best opportunities I could to develop and cultivate the faculties which God has bestowed on him, and which therefore, he holds under divine charter. . . . Having done this, I would leave him, as I would every other man, to find his level—to occupy the position to which he should be entitled by his intelligence and virtue."

True to his principles, Mann took a leading part in the congressional struggle over slavery. The issue was whether slavery should be permitted or prohibited in new states as they entered the Union. Feelings ran so high that fist fights and challenges to duels wound up more than one debate.

By 1852 Mann had had his fill of this bickering. When he was offered the presidency of a new college at Antioch, Ohio, he gladly accepted. At the age of fifty-seven Mann was setting out on a new adventure, uprooting his wife and children and parting from his friends.

Antioch was to be the fulfillment of all his dreams of improved education. He saw all the bright possibilities and none of the coming disappointments. Nor did he lose heart at his first sight of the "campus"—"one vast quagmire of clayey soil in which plank walks sank below the surface and in rainy weather floated upon it."

Antioch never became a large institution. At the start, it had a faculty of seven—two selected by Mann, the rest by the trustees. Tuition fees were to be kept to a minimum. Antioch was to be coeducational—a novelty at the time. In those days most men firmly believed that women were not intelligent enough to study mathematics and the sciences. Mann, who had no use for this view, insisted that all the students should take the same curriculum.

Soon the money problems which had always plagued Mann appeared once more. The college's finances were in rickety condition. The promised presidential salary dwindled to two-thirds, then to a half—and even that fraction was paid irregularly, or not at all.

In addition to his administrative and money-raising tasks, Mann had a heavy teaching schedule. To make ends meet, he lectured extensively in vacation time. There is little doubt that the pressures and anxieties of his work hastened his death in 1859.

Mann was one of those rare men whose influence is felt for decades and even centuries. The effect of his work is still stamped on our schools. In many ways he was ahead of his time—in his emphasis, for example, on teaching the sciences, which were sadly neglected in the schools of his day. He was one of the first to see the value of teaching spelling by word units rather than by single letters of the alphabet.

He astounded his contemporaries by insisting that the teacher must take an active, lively part in lessons instead of peering dully into a textbook and asking routine questions which call for memorized replies. Mann despised fear and physical punishment and competition as incentives to learning. The good teacher, in his opinion, would always know how to arouse the interest and affection of his pupils.

Mann stressed the value of demonstration, of example, of "visual aids" which play so large a role in our schools today. These were all innovations which filled his contemporaries with distrust. For Mann, the object of education was not to cram the student with received opinion, but rather to provide him with the means for forming his own reasoned views.

What Mann had to say about the problems of educating citizens in a democracy applies with even greater force in our own time. Take this passage from his July 4th oration of 1840:

"*All* must be wise and good or we must suffer the alternative of debasement and misery. It is not enough that a bare majority should be intelligent and upright. We need general intelligence and integrity as we need our daily bread."

In his annual report for 1844 he expressed the same thought with an even greater sense of urgency:

"If we do not prepare children to become good citizens;—if we do not develop their capacities, if we do not enrich their minds with knowledge, imbue their hearts with love of truth and duty, and a reverence for all things sacred and holy, then our republic must go down to destruction, as others have gone down before it; and mankind must sweep through another vast cycle of sin and suffering, before the dawn of a better era can arise upon the world. It is for our government, and for that public opinion, which, in a republic, governs the government, to choose between these alternatives of weal or woe."

It was doubtless such grim thoughts that inspired his famous concluding words to the Antioch class of 1859, a short time before his death:

"I beseech you to treasure up in your hearts these my parting words: Be ashamed to die until you have won some victory for humanity."

These words were chiseled on Horace Mann's tombstone.

RALPH WALDO EMERSON

Whoso would be a man, must be a nonconformist.

On his fifty-ninth birthday Ralph Waldo Emerson and his son Edward tried to bring a heifer into the barn. They pushed and tugged—with no result. The animal refused to budge. The sun was strong, the day was hot. The "Sage of Concord," who had been called "the wisest American," was baffled. Beads of sweat stood out on his forehead.

Finally an Irish servant girl came out. Smiling at the ineptitude of the men, she put a finger in the heifer's mouth. It followed her obediently, and with no trouble at all she brought it to its stall.

A trivial incident? Not for Emerson. He recorded it in his diary, and added: "I like people who can do things."

Very possibly one of the reasons why Emerson ad-

72

mired practical people was that he himself was a thinker, a bookish man, reflective, contemplative, fond of solitary strolls. He was very unhandy, and in our present age of incongruously mixed mechanization and "do-it-yourself" he would have been sadly helpless. Most practical tasks were beyond his skill. Occasionally he would do a little digging in his garden, for he felt it was good to be a man of the soil. But his little son Waldo was not fooled. "Look out, Father," he would say jokingly, "you'll dig your leg."

But what was much more important was that Emerson was the most widely admired American of his generation. Hermann Grimm, a famous German scholar of the day, put it very simply: "When I think of America, I think of you." Emerson was America's conscience, but not in any nagging way. Men felt ennobled and uplifted in his presence, and his writings had the same inspiring effect. For Emerson appealed to what was best in them, even though that best was neglected or hidden. That is why, despite the passage of time, Emerson still remains our most quoted and quotable writer.

Emerson's writings abound in short, pithy sentences that find answering echoes in our own minds. When he remarks that "nothing great was ever achieved without enthusiasm," we are reminded of our own mechanical thinking, our doubts, hesitations, and discouragements.

And when Emerson points out that "you find men talking everywhere from their memories, instead of from their own understanding," he is touching on a theme that was valid for his own age and for all ages. Think for yourself, he is forever telling his hearers and readers;

be your own man, come to your own conclusions, have the courage to defend them and act on them.

Sometimes the modernity of Emerson's criticisms of his own age is startling, as when he exclaims, "To what base uses we put this ineffable intellect! To reading all day murders and railway accidents, to choosing patterns for waistcoats and scarfs." And how telling this is: "I am ashamed to think how easily we capitulate to badges and names, to large societies and dead institutions."

But Emerson's general trend is by no means critical. He had the true poet's appreciation of the beauty of everyday things—a beauty that is lost on most of us because we are too deeply enmeshed in routine living. Emerson opens our eyes and lifts us to his own plane when he writes:

"And behold the sea, the opaline, plentiful and strong, yet beautiful as the rose and the rainbow, full of food, nourisher of men, purger of the world, creating a sweet climate, and, in its unchangeable ebb and flow, and in its beauty at a few furlongs, giving a hint of that which changes not, and is perfect."

Emerson teaches us to perceive more clearly, to live more vividly, to realize that seemingly trivial things can have profound meaning: "I embrace the common, I explore and sit at the feet of the familiar, the low." For Emerson nothing is finished or neatly rounded off; nothing stands still. Life is always becoming, changing, developing. It is a doctrine that appealed to the young people of his day, and it will never lose that magnetic quality.

"Give me insight into to-day," he writes exuberantly,

"and you may have the antique and future worlds."
A century later, a disillusioned American poet, appalled
by the economic misery of the 1930's, was to write that
"America was promises." True, Emerson would have
replied, but the promises were meant to be fulfilled not
by *America* but by *Americans*. Though he often knew
moments of discouragement, he never deceived himself
into thinking that solutions can be sought in the past.
As early as his twenty-first year he had written, "It is my
own humor to despise pedigree. I was educated to prize
it. . . . But the dead sleep in their moonless night; my
business is with the living."

Emerson's manner was so mild, so friendly, so cour-
teous, that people were shocked by the sturdy independence of his thinking. No traditional idea was safe from
his scrutiny. The well-worn grooves were not for him.
Even what was age-old took on new meaning as he re-
shaped it in a modernized form.

Ralph Waldo Emerson was born in Boston on May 25,
1803. His mother made a point of allowing him little
time outdoors and keeping him apart from other children. Indoors he was limited to the world of books. This
is why he grew up a shy, unworldly young man, a
stranger to practical matters and the social ease gained
from associating with other human beings. He was raised
to be an onlooker. Deeds, passions, all the joy and pain
of raw experience, were carefully kept from him.

He never ran, never laughed. The only strolling he
ever did as a child, he once remarked ruefully, was "from
book to book." Thus he acquired a taste for solitude

that remained with him all his life to some degree. It was only after years of struggling that Emerson developed his theory of compensation—the doctrine that whatever seems a defect, a burden, a misfortune to the heedless also contains some compensating good as well. "God has given me the seeing eye," he remarked, "but not the working hand." And yet he came to realize that by way of compensation for his lack of practical qualities, he was reflective, observant, penetrating, where most men are dull and heedless.

"Men are what their mothers made them," declared the mature Emerson, and we may be sure he was thinking of his own childhood when he wrote those words. He was a true son of the mother who had written to a friend that she loved living in the country, far from the "useless ceremony, parade, and pomp" of city life. In later years, whenever he left the serene peace of his beloved Concord for a short visit to Boston, he could not help feeling a touch of that suspicion and contempt that is the natural reaction of any simple rustic.

Mrs. Emerson retired every morning to pray and meditate. She kept a supply of knitting on hand to accompany every conversation, for it seemed sinful in her eyes to spend her time on mere talk. Though she was sweet-natured, she was a firm believer in discipline and she disapproved of any open show of affection. We can see traces of her influence in Emerson's observation that "no man would consent to live in society if he was obliged to admit everybody to his house that chose to come."

Mrs. Emerson had no great hopes for Waldo's future, for he lacked concentration. His childhood habit of sucking his thumb distressed her, so she had him wear a mitten to cure him of the habit.

Waldo's father was a scholar, with a scholar's love of books. He was a fun-loving man, fond of music and good company—"faults" for which he contritely reproached himself. This led him to be a stern disciplinarian with his children. All the Emerson children were frail. Three of Waldo's brothers, as well as his sister, died young. The remaining brother was a harmless mental defective. The father died at the comparatively early age of forty-two.

Waldo's ancestors had lived in New England since 1635, when the first of the line, a minister, left England for Massachusetts because he refused to conform to the strict doctrines laid down in those uneasy times by the Church of England. Eight generations of ministers had followed him down the centuries—men whose lives had had the same bookish, withdrawn, sedate, indoor pattern that had such a profound influence on Waldo.

As a boy of ten Waldo spent three hours a day on Latin in the Boston Latin School. Then he devoted two hours to arithmetic in another school, but he had so much trouble with figures that he often played truant. His schoolwork bored him, and he was a poor pupil. Whenever possible, he stole a few moments reading a novel or writing poetry—and never regretted it.

Emerson's maiden aunt, Mary Moody Emerson, was a vigorous, restless woman with a fine mind, unconventional ideas, and a taste for philosophy and interesting conversation. She encouraged Waldo, her favorite nephew, spurred his ambition and started the process which turned the repressed child into a fearlessly independent thinker.

In his graduating year, at the age of fourteen, Waldo was described as quite tall for his age, with a pale complexion, blue eyes, and "Saxon blond" hair. His manner was noticeably grave and reserved. Always calm and quiet, he never revealed his emotions. His schoolmates found in him a mingling of "shyness, awkwardness, and dignity."

The early death of Waldo's father had left the Emerson family in straitened circumstances. Waldo earned his way through Harvard as a messenger and waiter. These unhappy years left him with a "goading, soul-sickening sense of extreme poverty." The dull college teaching of those days had little appeal for him. For a long time he kept to himself, made no friends, and his real education was derived from books of his own choosing which he read in solitude.

Waldo's friends were Shakespeare, Milton, Plato, and other classics. What he read in those years shaped the rest of his life. There are hints in his later writings of his loneliness in college— "Archery, cricket, gun and fishing rod, horse and boat, are all educators, liberalizers; and so are dancing, dress, and the street talk." It is no accident that he lists activities which were all absent from his youth.

Some of Waldo's shrinking from youthful pleasures was not of his own choosing. For example, though he read many plays, he never attended an actual theatrical performance. Such attendance, if discovered, brought a Harvard student a ten-dollar fine from the college.

It took Waldo almost two years to make the first timid

approaches to social contacts with his fellow students. He enjoyed the experiment and later commented, "You send your child to the schoolmaster, but it is the schoolboys who educate him."

One of these new contacts was to have important consequences. When Waldo joined a reading circle that subscribed to the leading British magazines, he suddenly discovered that the world of his own time contained living poets who were blazing new trails and were not content with chewing over ideas and techniques that had been recorded hundreds or even thousands of years ago. It was his first tentative approach to what was to become one of his basic ideas—that each generation must hew out its own achievements, instead of contenting itself with what had been done and thought in earlier times.

Waldo's interest in these exciting influences was not in line with his intention to become a minister. "Intention" is too strong a word; actually, like many gifted but undecided youngsters, he did not know what he wanted to be. He did know that the ministry held only feeble attraction for him; but, like his father, he was allowing himself to be persuaded into a career about which he was lukewarm.

Troubled by his uncertainty and his will-less drift into an unexciting career, he criticized himself mercilessly. "All around me are industrious and will be great," he writes in his journal at the age of seventeen. "I am indolent and will be insignificant."

And twelve days before his nineteenth birthday, he takes stock in an entry which is even bleaker: "I have not the kind affections of a pigeon. Ungenerous and selfish, cautious and cold, I yet wish to be romantic; have not sufficient feeling to speak a natural, hearty welcome to a friend or stranger." Yet despite this youthful unhappiness and family griefs that would have crushed many another man, he eventually achieved a hard-won serenity that gave him the title of "the Sage of Concord."

During the winter vacation the young man earned a little money by teaching. But he hated the work and wrote despairingly of the "hot, steaming, stoved, stinking, dirty, A-B spelling-school-room." He completed his college course without distinction, ending up a mediocre thirtieth in a class of fifty-nine. His grades were not good enough for membership in the Phi Beta Kappa Society—an ironic point when one considers the tremendous stir created by his speech years later to Harvard's Phi Beta Kappa chapter. (This address is described on page 88.) Lacking abilities, as he thought, for any other career, he was headed for the ministry.

The following year young Emerson became a teacher in a school for young ladies, run by his brother William. To be in the presence of the girls was an ordeal, but he needed the money to help his younger brother through college and the Harvard Divinity School. He felt he had nothing to look forward to, and alternated between self-pity and self-contempt. Sadly he noted that "there is not in the whole Universe of God one being to whom I am attached with warm and ideal devotion."

Like his friend Thoreau, to whom another chapter of this book is devoted, Emerson disapproved of severe punishment—a form of self-restraint that seemed eccentric in those days. Emerson's idea of punishment was to have the students read a passage from Plutarch's *Lives* of the greatest men of ancient Greece and Rome. This cannot have done the pupils any harm and may have done them some good. It was no doubt from his lifelong reading of Plutarch that Emerson derived his strong conviction that the spirit of an age expresses itself through the achievements of its great men.

Emerson's health had been poor and his physician, thinking he might be in the opening phase of tuberculosis, sent him to Florida for his health. One day in St. Augustine he attended a meeting of a Bible society whose treasurer happened to be the marshal of the district. Through some colossal thoughtlessness he had set the society's session in a yard adjoining a slave auction. Both events—the Bible society meeting and the slave auction—went on at the same time, within earshot of each other.

So "one ear therefore heard the glad tidings of great joy," Emerson wrote, "whilst the other was regaled with 'Going, gentlemen, going!' And almost without changing our position we might aid in sending the Scriptures into Africa, or bid for 'four children without the mother' who had been kidnapped therefrom." This acid comment foreshadows Emerson's passionate involvement later on with the slavery problem.

With his health greatly improved, Emerson returned to Boston. In 1826 he was admitted to the ministry, but he was still at odds with himself, for he knew that he had no real vocation for such a career. His life brightened when he met Ellen Tucker, a beautiful girl with whom he fell in love. But she died of tuberculosis a few years after their marriage, and in the shock of his grief Emerson at last left the ministry in 1832, after a public declaration that he could not accept certain doctrines of his church.

Believing that a change of scene would soften the impact of Emerson's grief, his friends raised a sum to send him to Europe. On Christmas Day of 1832 he left for the Old World in search of fresh impressions and ideas. Perhaps in meeting his literary idols and in studying the art treasures produced over a period of centuries, he would find in the Old World what he had missed in the New. But he was destined to be disappointed. In Italy and France Emerson was taken aback by the blend of beauty and poverty. There was too much crowding, too much dirt, too much preoccupation with the past.

In England, too, he was disappointed in his meetings with the writers he had admired. Like others before him and since, he made the disconcerting discovery that many a book is more admirable than the man who wrote it.

Only Thomas Carlyle, despite his rather sour criticisms and violent turns of speech, came up to Emerson's expectations. Carlyle, already a famous man, was to capture the imagination of the reading public with his history of the French Revolution; his grim, colorful, and sardonic picture of the great upheaval was to be taken as a warning that time was running out for essential social reforms in England.

What bound Carlyle and Emerson together was that both, frail as they were, admired great men of action.

Carlyle's hero was Frederick the Great, while Napoleon was Emerson's idol. There was this all-important difference: Carlyle cynically gloated over Frederick's unprovoked attacks on neighboring countries; Emerson— who appreciated to the full Napoleon's military genius, his statesmanship, his personal magnetism, his flexibility of judgment—was unsparing in his criticism of the darker sides of Napoleon's career.

Although Emerson and Carlyle met on only one other occasion, many years later, they remained lifelong friends through the medium of a lively correspondence. While Emerson often alluded to the unforgettable impression made on him by Carlyle, he was too modest to describe Carlyle's reaction.

It must have required a man of singular sweetness of character to charm the dour, touchy Carlyle, but that is apparently just what the unknown young American did, judging from Mrs. Carlyle's recollections: "I should never forget the Visitor, who years ago in the Desert descended on us, out of the clouds as it were, and made one day there look like enchantment for us, and left me weeping that it was only *one* day."

Finally, after eight months of European travel, Emerson was homeward bound in September, 1833, watching "the last lump of England recede without regret." His disappointment in Europe might have made the whole trip a wasted experience; instead, it had a profoundly creative effect.

For the first time the homesick, thirty-year-old Emerson was able to appreciate his own country. "We go to Europe," he wrote whimsically, obviously relishing the paradox, "to be Americanized." With newly gained confidence and self-reliance he could say, "I am thankful I am an American."

Back home, he learned that the settlement of his wife's estate had left him with an income that would relieve his money worries. His brain was busy with ideas for books, and his new career of lecturing gave him enjoyable contacts with his fellow Americans. In 1834 he bought the house at Concord where he was to spend the rest of his life; and the following year he married Lydia Jackson. Their tranquil and affectionate relationship was marred only by the tragic death, at the age of five, of Waldo, his favorite child.

Concord was a pleasant, restful town with a lovely countryside. The memory of the famous Revolutionary battle of Concord fired Emerson's imagination—his house was almost within sight of "the rude bridge that arched the flood" where "once the embattled farmers stood/And fired the shot heard round the world." If America was still promises, then the battle of Concord was the first word of those promises and served to remind Emerson that he must do what he could to make those promises come true.

Nor did Emerson live in rustic stagnation, for his neighbors included some of the most famous men of the day—Henry Thoreau, Nathaniel Hawthorne, and Bronson Alcott. Thoreau was only twenty-one when he and Emerson first met. They were much taken with each other. Emerson said: "I am familiar with his thoughts; they are mine, quite originally dressed." Thoreau often assisted him, spent much time with the Emerson children, and worked around the house and garden, for he was as skillful with his hands as Emerson was inept. In later years there were times when their friendship cooled —naturally enough in the case of such thoroughgoing individualists.

Emerson's deep contentment in Concord is often mirrored in his writings. He was slyly teasing his money-grubbing countrymen when he wrote, "The charming landscape which I saw this morning is indubitably made up of twenty or thirty farms. Miller owns this field, Locke that, and Manning the woodland beyond. But none of them own the landscape." And in the same vein he could say, "When I bought my farm, I did not know what a bargain I had in the bluebirds, bobolinks, and thrushes; as little did I know what sublime mornings and sunsets I was buying."

Perhaps he was having a quiet laugh at the expense of the land speculators who were to bring on the dreadful Panic of 1837 by frantically buying and selling plots they had never seen and which perhaps did not even exist—a process that was to be repeated ninety years later, with even more disastrous results, by their descendants in the speculation in underwater "lots" off the Florida coast. Emerson pitied them as they unheedingly passed beauty by, and he might have asked them in the words of Richard Owen Cambridge, a forgotten eighteenth-century writer:

> *What is the worth of anything,*
> *But for the happiness 'twill bring?*

But Emerson's private happiness did not blind him to
the evils of his time. He was not the man to conclude,
on a note of resignation, that nothing remained but to
cultivate one's garden. To his way of thinking, his fellow Americans were timid, dull, and interested in nothing but money. When Charles Dickens visited the United
States, he was chiefly "impressed by the prevailing seri-
ousness and melancholy air of business; which was so
general and unvarying, that at every new town I came
to, I seemed to meet the very same people whom I had
left behind at the last." De Tocqueville, the brilliant
French observer, went to even greater extremes, assert-
ing that the Americans were people "who in civilization
and enlightenment love only what is useful to well-
being, and who shut themselves in the American soli-
tudes with an axe and some newspapers."

Emerson saw little hope in political activity. Political
figures were uninspired and often corrupt. He recalled
an orator who had "wittily compared our party promises to western roads, which opened stately enough,
with planted trees on either side to tempt the traveller,
but soon became narrower and ended in a squirrel-track
, and ran up a tree." It was not always easy to remain
urbane, and when Daniel Webster betrayed the anti-
slavery forces to further his presidential ambitions,
Emerson lashed out at him with an uncharacteristically
savage poem in which every word stung like a whip.

Not a day passed without some cruel wrong to the Indians. The Mexican War struck him as a shameless land
grab. Slavery was an acid eating away at the nation's
integrity. Before every thinking man there loomed the

coming civil war. With sweeping bitterness Emerson proclaimed that from 1790 to 1820 Massachusetts had produced "not a word, a speech, a conversation, or a thought."

There was this difference in the attitudes of Emerson and the visitors from the Old World: they took gloomy satisfaction in the decline of the country that had once been hailed as a Promised Land. But Emerson, because he loved his country, wanted to remold it nearer the heart's desire. Evil was a challenge—something to resist, not something to submit to.

Some Emerson critics have accused him of complacency. Apparently they never read such hard-hitting words as these:

"Because our education is defective, because we are superficial and ill-read, we are forced to make the most of that position, of ignorance. Hence America is a vast know-nothing party, and we disparage books, and cry up intuition."

The age, like all ages, was not bad; it was good *and* bad. Evil was inextricably tangled up in the world's web. There was the same confusion, the same blend of the hopeful and the menacing, that Dickens pictured in the exuberant opening of *A Tale of Two Cities* devoted to the eve of the French Revolution: "It was the best of times, it was the worst of times, it was the age of wisdom, it was the age of foolishness, it was the epoch of belief, it was the epoch of incredulity, it was the season of Darkness, it was the season of Light, it was the spring of hope, it was the winter of despair, we had everything before us, we had nothing before us, we were all going direct to

Heaven, we were all going direct the other way. . . ."

So Emerson did not despair. "What is man born for," he asked, "but to be a Reformer, a Remaker of what man has made?" Viewing the stirrings of social reform all about him, Emerson noted with genial exaggeration that every reading man "has the draft of a new community in his waistcoat pocket."

Emerson published his first book, *Nature*, in 1836. In this brief but thought-packed volume, and still under the influence of his European experiences, he called on America to develop a new poetry, a new philosophy. "Why should we grope among the dry bones of the past?" After all, "there are new lands, new men, new thoughts." But his demand was too bold, and few Americans paid any attention to the book.

The Panic of 1837 made a deep impression on Emerson. It saddened him to see how engrossed his countrymen were in making money, in "getting ahead," in enslaving themselves to "some barking and bellowing institution." He felt he could show them the way to a nobler life. Speaking to a receptive audience of Harvard students the same year, he delivered the memorable Phi Beta Kappa address that made him a famous man.

First he paid his respects to the scholar, whom he glorified as "man thinking." But, he went on, "the spirit of the American freeman is already suspected to be timid, imitative, tame. The scholar is decent, indolent, complaisant. The mind of this country, taught to aim at low objects, eats upon itself. There is no work for any but the decorous and the complaisant."

American subservience to the Old World had to come

to an end sooner or later. "Our day of dependence, our long apprenticeship to the learning of other lands, draws to a close." The scholar could not remain a narrow specialist—he would need a broader culture and would have to seek out the world of ideas and action.

Becoming self-reliant, he could serve his own age and his own country; he would nevertheless be allied with all humanity, for all mankind was linked by a common fate and a common living process. Because America had a democratic basis, it offered more to the individual and made him really important. There was no longer any reason for the American to be timidly overwhelmed by the achievements of other countries. It was time for Americans to make their distinctive contribution to world culture.

"Meek young men," he said, "grow up in libraries, believing it their duty to accept the views" formed by the great men of olden times. But they forgot that these great men "were only young men in libraries when they wrote these books." Then, returning to his advice to the too bookish scholars, he resumed, "Action is with the scholar subordinate, but it is essential. Without it he is not yet man. Without it thought can never ripen into truth. . . . Only so much do I know, as I have lived. Instantly we know whose words are loaded with life, and whose not."

At the same time, he warned, let the scholar have confidence in himself: "Let him not quit his belief that a popgun is a popgun, though the ancient and honorable of the earth affirm it to be the crack of doom."

Young people took in Emerson's words avidly, while

their elders were outraged. So great was the scandal that at the height of his fame twenty-eight years passed before Emerson was again invited to speak at Harvard. Like Socrates in ancient Greece, Emerson in his quiet way had become a gadfly, intent on driving men out of the ancient, smooth-worn grooves and calling on them to be independent, fearless, and self-reliant.

In another address at Dartmouth College, Emerson was even franker. "You will hear that the first duty is to get land and money, place and name. 'What is this truth you seek? What is this beauty?' men will ask with derision."

Some of them, Emerson told the students, would reply, "I must eat the good of the land, and let learning and romantic expectations go, until a more convenient time." But in that case, Emerson warned his young listeners, "then dies the man in you; then once more perish the buds of art, and poetry, and science, as they have perished already in a thousand thousand men." These eloquent speeches prove why Emerson appealed so strongly to the young people of his generation, and why he will continue to appeal to the young people of every generation.

Although Emerson found public controversy distasteful, there were times when he had to raise his voice against cruelty and greed. Such an occasion arose when the Cherokee Indians were forced off their ancestral lands in Georgia and sent against their will to Oklahoma. On this "Trail of Tears" a third of them perished.

Emerson was ashamed for his country. Indignantly he wrote to President Van Buren, "Such a dereliction of faith and virtue, such a denial of justice, and such deafness to screams of mercy were never heard in times of peace and in the dealings of a nation with its own allies and wards, since the earth was made."

But nothing could stop the exile of the Indians. For, as Emerson memorably put it, "Things are in the saddle and ride mankind." He looked for a conversion of the whole man, for he felt that the world would never improve as long as mankind remained selfish, greedy, cruel, cowardly, envious, and lazy. He had neither the relentless intensity nor the narrow-minded rigidity that marks the fanatical reformer. Emerson relished the richness and variety of human life too much to pin his faith to the men of one fixed idea who wanted to "pull up lilies and plant skunk cabbages in their places." History offers many examples of narrow-minded dictators who replaced beauty and some freedom with ugliness and much regimentation.

And when Emerson attended a meeting of the Friends of Universal Progress, he commented wryly that "if the assembly was disorderly, it was picturesque. Madmen, madwomen, men with beards, Muggletonians, Come-outers, Groaners, Agrarians, Seventh-Day Baptists, Quakers, Abolitionists, Calvinists, Unitarians, and philosophers." And each was certain that he was the only one who had the cure for the world's ills.

But skepticism was no solution either. Perhaps he could make a beginning toward curing the world's ills in his own household by asking his maid and his cook, as a democratic gesture, to eat all their meals together with the family. But both servants were so shocked by this daring suggestion that they begged off more or less tactfully.

Emerson had to acknowledge himself beaten. "I have not yet conquered my own house," he wrote with delightful self-mockery. "It irks me and repents me. Shall I raise the siege of this hencoop, and march away to a pretended siege of Babylon?"

So he tried another approach to the democratic ideal. Like the common run of humanity, he would work with his hands. But he was clumsy and utterly unsuited to manual labor. It did not take long for his garden to require expert treatment. Emerson had many admirable qualities, but a green thumb was not one of them. He concluded that "if a man own land, the land owns him."

As Emerson approached middle age, solitude was losing much of its charm for him. The earnings from his books and lectures left him in fairly comfortable circumstances. Family life was pleasant, and under its mellowing effect he began to find congenial qualities in his Concord neighbors. He helped to organize a library for the town. He dutifully served as a volunteer fireman, and he studied democracy in action at town meetings. From this time on, his journals were studded with ideas suggested by the pithy remarks of his Concord acquaintances. Besides being the mainstay of his income, Emerson's annual winter lectures helped him in other ways. Many of them turned out to be the material of subsequent books. Above all, he was enthralled by the vastness and variety of his country, he enjoyed meeting new people, visiting a town for the first time, gaining new insights, widening his horizon. Then, after these enlivening encounters, it was all the sweeter to return to the quiet of Concord and the serenity of home.

Freed of the torturing doubts of his youth, he was happy . . . or at least, he might have been, if his preoccupation with the issue of slavery had not continued to trouble him more and more. "This calamity darkens my days," he wrote in his journal. His feeling about slavery was so intense that when one of his children was writing a school composition on building a house, he told the child gravely that every house should be built with a space in it to hide a runaway slave.

In 1844 a meeting was held at the Concord Court House to celebrate the tenth anniversary of Great Britain's freeing of its West Indian slaves. Emerson, as the town's leading citizen, was invited to deliver the principal address of the evening. His speech on this occasion is worth studying in some detail, as it reveals how he felt about slavery and is perhaps the most powerful single attack ever made on it.

He started by showing how readily moral sloth reconciled itself to slavery. "The sugar they raised was excellent; nobody tasted blood in it. The coffee was fragrant; the tobacco was incense; the brandy made nations happy; the cotton clothed the world. What! all raised by these men, and no wages? Excellent! What a convenience! They seemed created by Providence to bear the heat and the whippings, and make these fine articles."

But Emerson's probing mind analyzed more than the economic evils of slavery. "The planter is the spoiled child of his unnatural habits, and has contracted in his indolent and luxurious climate the need of excitement by irritating and tormenting his slave."

He shrewdly demonstrated that even from the point of view of sheer self-interest, slavery harmed the white population as well:

"Slavery is no scholar, no improver; it does not love the whistle of the railroad; it does not love the newspaper; the mail-bag, a college, a book or a preacher who has the absurd whim of saying what he thinks; it does not increase the white population; it does not improve the soil; everything goes to decay."

All this was clear to Emerson, the "unrealistic" philosopher who was supposed to have his head in the clouds. But "realistic" and "practical" people were blind to these drawbacks of slavery.

Turning to slavery in his own country, Emerson lashed out at the Massachusetts Senators and Representatives in Washington, who, with the glorious exception of John Quincy Adams, "sit dumb at their desks." He dismissed them scornfully as "accomplished lawyers and merchants, and very eloquent at dinners and caucuses." But, he added bitingly, "there is a disastrous want of *men* from New England."

True to his conception of mankind as an inseparable community, he closed on this note: "It is a doctrine alike of the oldest and the newest philosophy, that man is one, and that you cannot injure any member, without a sympathetic injury to all the members."

And the reaction in the South? His words found no answering echoes. "His mind is like a rag-picker's basket," the *Southern Literary Messenger* commented disdainfully, "full of all manner of trash."

When Congress passed the Fugitive Slave Law in 1851, Emerson spoke up boldly against it. This act required every American, even in those states where slavery had been abolished, to return any runaway slave he might meet. "This is a law," Emerson told his fellow citizens, "which every one of you will break on the earliest occasion."

Three years later, at a great mass meeting held in New York City to discuss the abominable law, Emerson was again the principal speaker. He started his speech in apologetic vein. "I do not often speak to public questions —they are odious and hurtful, and it seems like meddling or leaving your work."

But as he warmed to his theme he shamed the backsliders, and the easygoing and indifferent who were spinelessly accepting a monstrous evil. He reminded them of "the coldness and indifferentism of scholars and literary men. They are lovers of liberty in Greece and Rome and in the English Commonwealth, but they are lukewarm lovers of the liberty of America in 1854."

Then he turned to the statesmen who supported slavery—"brilliant men, accomplished men, men of high station, a President of the United States, Senators, men of eloquent speech, but men without self-respect, without character." And he added bluntly: "It was strange to see that office, age, fame, talent, even a repute for honesty, count for nothing." Sternly he brought them to account: "If slavery is good, then is lying, theft, arson, homicide, each and all good."

The tension of the antislavery struggle had reached such a point as early as 1847 that Emerson was glad to slip away for his second visit to England for a series of lectures. He was received with an enthusiasm that filled every hall to capacity. A listener named Crabb Robinson gave his reaction in these words: "It was with a feeling of predetermined dislike that I had the curiosity to look at Emerson at Northampton's, a fortnight ago; when, in an instant, all my dislike vanished. He has one of the most interesting countenances I ever beheld—a combination of sweetness and intelligence that quite disarmed me."

Another listener left this striking description of Emerson: "The thinness of his body, accentuated by his nearly six feet of height, would make him look fragile in comparison with the solidly built Britons, and their vitality would awaken his envy. But in spite of the narrow and sharply sloping shoulders on which it was set, his head gave the impression of firmness. His shock of brown hair, now darker than in his youth, and his short, unobtrusive side whiskers partly framed a face with rugged features and penetrating blue eyes. Sometimes, perhaps commonly, his face had a luminous, friendly expression revealing an unusual combination of sensitiveness and self-control."

Most lecturers approach their work in a perfunctory spirit, content with trifling variations on the same theme year after year. Not so Emerson. "When you come to write Lyceum lectures," he admonishes himself in his journal, "remember that you are not to say, What must be said in a Lyceum? but, What discoveries or stimulating thoughts have I to impart to a thousand persons?"

As an old man, he looked back over his lecturing and

writing career and wondered what it had accomplished. On the surface, not much. "I have been writing and speaking what were once called novelties, for twenty-five or thirty years, and have not one disciple." Did this disturb Emerson? Not at all. He continues:

"Why? Not that what I said was not true; not that it has not found intelligent receivers; but because it did not go from any wish in me to bring men to me, but to themselves." Emerson's lifework can be summed up in this phrase: *to bring men to themselves.* "I delight in driving them from me. What could I do if they came to me?—they would interrupt and encumber me. This is my boast that I have no school follower. I should account it a measure of the impurity of insight, if it did not create independence."

We have no way of knowing whether Emerson realized how closely his audiences related his words to his personality. Some, perhaps many, were uplifted by his presence even though they did not share his thoughts. A scrubwoman who never missed any of his Concord lectures was asked whether she understood them. "Not a word," she replied, "but I like to see him stand there and look as though he thought everyone was as good as he was." If Emerson gave such an impression, it was from his radiance of sheer goodness and not from condescension. If we analyze this woman's words, we see that she instinctively grasped Emerson's doctrine: his insistence on the unique worth of every human being and his concept of mankind as an inseparable community.

More articulate listeners, like James Russell Lowell,

one of the leading American poets of the day, conveyed the same reaction in more sophisticated language:

"We used to walk in from the country to the Masonic Temple (I think it was), through the crisp winter night, and listen to that thrilling voice of his, so charged with subtle meaning and subtle music, as shipwrecked men on a raft to the hail of a ship that came with unhoped-for food and rescue.

"He boggled, he lost his place, he had to put on his glasses; but it was as if a creature from some fairer world had lost his way in our fogs, and it was *our* fault, not his."

Unlike last night's already forgotten television program, the impression made by Emerson never faded. "The only firebrand of my youth," Justice Oliver Wendell Holmes wrote in his old age, "that burns to me as brightly as ever, is Emerson."

Another old man, George William Curtis, recalled an Emerson lecture he had attended as a boy. It was given on a sparkling winter night in a small Sunday-school room lit up by flickering oil light and heated by a pot-bellied stove.

"All laughed at the delightful humor or the illustrative anecdote that sparkled for a moment upon the surface of his talk; and some sat inspired with unknown resolves, soaring upon lofty hopes as they heard. A nobler life, a better manhood, a purer purpose, wooed every listening soul. It was not argument, nor description, nor appeal. It was wit and wisdom, and hard sense and poetry, and scholarship and music."

Emerson's life was darkened by many personal trag-edies—the early deaths of his brothers, his father, his first wife, his favorite child. By the time he had found his true vocation, after years of drifting, he had passed his thirtieth birthday. It was from his grief and his aimlessness, and not from books, that he developed his theories of compensation and self-reliance.

Emerson felt there was something of the divine in every living creature—but that "something" was trapped in routine living and thinking. As he looked around him at the meaningless bustle and energetic struggles of other men, they gave him the impression of really being asleep: the godlike element in them slumbered even though they gave the appearance of feverish activity. They were absorbed in petty details and dull activities; they were timid, shallow, and im-itative.

Emerson boldly told them to be themselves, to think for themselves, instead of conforming to this or that current mode. Each man, he realized, has some special ability or skill or interest through which he can best express himself. Let him follow his bent, and pay less attention to the world's opinion. Then he would no longer feel "pinched in a corner," as Emerson put it.

It is the happy paradox of Emerson's thinking that although it has a universal appeal, it encourages each individual to be his own unique self. For, as his friend Hermann Grimm expressed it, "You write so that everyone reading your words must think that you had thought of him alone."

WILLIAM LLOYD
GARRISON

I will be as harsh as truth and as uncompromising as
justice. On this subject I do not wish to speak or write
with moderation. I am in earnest, I will not equivocate;
I will not excuse; I will not retreat a single inch—and
I will be heard.

The Massachusetts town of Newburyport, on the mouth
of the Merrimack River and not far from Boston, is
an industrial center. Such humdrum products as shoes
and silverware have replaced Newburyport's activities
in the old clipper days.

As you walk along High Street you can still see some
of the stately mansions of the men who became wealthy
from shipping, whaling, shipbuilding—and privateering;
for Newburyport, as the name indicates, was once
a leading seaport.

When you are tired of sightseeing, you can turn
around and walk back, past the center of town, until
you come to a weatherbeaten statue in a quiet, sunlit
square. It is the statue of Newburyport's most famous
son, and the serenity of the peaceful scene contrasts

weirdly with the course of his turbulent life. Today, Newburyport's romantic past is forgotten by all except a few antiquarians, but the town is remembered as the birthplace of William Lloyd Garrison. Although nearly a century has passed since Garrison died in 1879, the ideas for which he fought so bravely or so cantankerously—the choice of the adverb depends on your point of view—are still very much with us.

When foreigners visited the United States in the years before the Civil War, they were struck by a glaring paradox. They could not understand how America could pride itself on being the home of liberty and at the same time tolerate Negro slavery.

Charles Dickens, for example, who visited this country in 1842, was outraged by the spectacle of Negro slavery. Writing about a trip through Virginia, he describes a pitiful scene on the train:

"In the negro car belonging to the train in which we made this journey were a mother and her children who had just been purchased; the husband and father being left behind with their old owner. The children cried the whole way, and the mother was misery's picture."

Dickens goes on to list a good many advertisements that appeared in newspapers of the period. Here are two of the less harrowing items:

"Committed to jail, a man who calls his name John. He has a clog of iron on his right foot which will weigh four or five pounds."

"Ran away, a negro woman and two children. A few days before she went off I burnt her with a hot iron

on the left side of her face. I tried to make the letter
M.''

Is it any wonder that Garrison fought slavery with
every means at his command?

William Lloyd Garrison was born in Newburyport
in 1805, in the house where George Whitefield, the
famous Methodist preacher, had died thirty-five years
earlier. The newborn infant was to grow up to become
an even more eloquent preacher.

Few childhoods have been more unhappy. The elder
Garrison, a sailor, took to drink and, when William was
three years old, deserted his family and was never heard
from again.

The Garrison children were brought up in the greatest
poverty. Sometimes the fatherless boy took a tin pail
to wealthy people's homes to gather leftovers. Other
times he simply went hungry.

His schoolmates baited him because of his poverty.
A callous schoolmaster "cured" him of lefthandedness
by rapping him on the knuckles whenever he wrote with
his left hand. The troubled boy was backward in his
studies, and naturally enough he found it hard to make
friends.

At the age of nine his schooldays were over: he was
apprenticed to a shoemaker. The work was too much
for a child, and he was lonesome and bored. Later he
was apprenticed to a cabinetmaker, but after six weeks
he ran away.

After the boy was brought back, he was apprenticed
a third time—as a printer's helper in the office of the

Newburyport *Herald*. This proved to be a decisive turn-ing-point in his life, for he found the work congenial. In setting type he was accurate, conscientious, and fascinated not only by the type but by the meaning of the words.

When he was ten years old he had his first glimpse of slavery when he saw handcuffed Negroes being led to the wharves to be shipped to an unknown destination. Whether this incident left a lasting impression, we do not know; many years were to pass before he began his attacks on slavery.

As he became more and more interested in newspaper articles, his innate love of fine writing began to assert itself. Soon he was spending his evenings reading master-pieces of English literature. He joined a debating society, became a faithful churchgoer, and began to take an intelligent interest in politics. He was at last finding his proper level and making up for his lost schooling.

By the time he was seventeen, he began writing his own articles under the pen-name of "An Old Bachelor." The articles were so well received that he revealed his identity to the editor and continued writing under his own name. Soon the young man was promoted to be foreman of the print shop.

In 1826, when Garrison was twenty-one, he started his own paper, with a rather conservative point of view that gave no hint of his future fire-eating journalism.

The paper lasted only six months. Young Garrison returned to printing for a while, and then assumed the editorship of the *National Philanthropist*, a Baptist organ dedicated to the crusade against drinking. Garrison's style was now much more vigorous; but he was still very respectful to the powers that be, and his references to the "peculiar institution" of slavery were scanty.

About this time the young man turned to public speaking. On the platform he was much more outspoken than in his newspaper views. Instead of joining in the tributes to Thomas Jefferson and John Adams, who had both died on July 4, 1826, Garrison contemptuously dismissed the "rhapsodies upon the deeds of our fathers."

Not that he despised those great men. But he was speaking for his own generation: he was already aware that the good fight must be fought anew in every generation, and that the Americans of 1826 could not smugly pride themselves on the laurels won by the Americans of 1776.

The fierce fight over the Missouri Compromise in 1820 had made it clear to all thoughtful Americans that slavery would lead to bitter dissension between South and North.

The South's position was clear. Slavery, in the words of a Charleston paper, was "the great source of their prosperity, wealth, and happiness." From this it was only a step to conclude that slavery was actually good for the slave as well as for the master, and that slavery was ordained of God.

We take it for granted that the attitude of the North was equally uncompromising in opposing slavery; but this does not give us a true picture of the period. In any age, many people are indifferent to the great political issues of the day and prefer not to be disturbed by troublesome problems.

It is true that some religious groups, notably the Quakers, were strongly opposed to slavery. Other religious organizations ignored the issues, while some even went so far as to actively endorse slavery. The Northern owners of textile mills and other businessmen who made money from cotton defended slavery vociferously. They bluntly recommended rough treatment for all anti-slavery agitators.

Even the Northern workingman, who might have been expected to sympathize with the victims of slavery, was often strongly anti-Negro. For he tended to take the view that the Negroes, if freed, would compete for jobs, thereby creating unemployment for whites and dragging down wage scales which were on a low level to begin with.

Even in New England, which we think of as the hotbed of abolitionist sentiment, there were outbreaks against Negroes. In the 1840's, when the abolitionists had already gained considerable ground, a segregated school for colored children in Salem had to be discontinued because of threats of violence. In Canaan, New Hampshire, a mob of three hundred people yoked a hundred oxen to tear down the Noyes Academy because it admitted a few Negro pupils. In Plainfield, Connecticut, Prudence Crandall was arrested because she admitted a colored girl to her private school. She was forbidden by her pastor to attend church services; physicians refused to treat members of her family; and her house was wrecked.

Nor did the outbreak of the Civil War completely modify this attitude. At an antislavery meeting in Boston held during the war, Ralph Waldo Emerson was hooted off the platform when he tried to speak out against slavery. In New York, after the National Conscription Act was passed in 1863, uncontrollable mobs ran amuck, destroying property, looting, capturing an armory for rifles and ammunition, killing any Negroes and known abolitionists they could lay their hands on. One of the buildings destroyed was a Negro orphanage, and hundreds of children were left without shelter. The Seventh Regiment had to be rushed back to the city from Gettysburg—ten days after the great battle!—and with the help of police, militia, naval forces, and cadets from West Point, managed to subdue the rioters after a week-long struggle. It is estimated that the fury of the mob resulted in a thousand casualties and almost two million dollars' worth of property damage.

It must be remembered, too, that behind the arguments of Southern apologists, with their learned references to Plato and Aristotle and their pious quotations from the Bible, there lurked the implied threat of physical violence. Thus, William C. Preston, United States Senator from South Carolina, stated frankly:

"Let an abolitionist come within the borders of South Carolina, if we can catch him, we will try him, and notwithstanding all the influence of all the governments on earth, including the Federal Government, we will hang him."

The open lawlessness of this statement, all the more shocking from an officer of the United States government, was not calculated to make Garrison write with sweetness and light. In fact, he sturdily commented that the cause of abolition would not flourish until "it excites popular tumult, and brings down upon it a shower of brickbats, and rotten eggs, and is threatened with a coat of tar-and-feathers."

These words were written by Garrison when he had become the acknowledged leader of the antislavery forces. But even in one of his earliest speeches in 1826 he expressed his contempt in devastating words for the Americans of his day who prided themselves on the Declaration of Independence and looked on smugly at the degrading spectacle of slavery:

"I am ashamed of my country. I am sick of the unmeaning declarations in praise of liberty and equality; of our hypocritical cant about the inalienable rights of man."

With characteristic frankness Garrison had taken his stand against slavery; but it was not until he met the Quaker Benjamin Lundy that he decided to devote all his efforts to emancipation. Lundy was no "wild-eyed radical." As a gentle preacher of truly Christian ethics, he sought no violent overthrow of the hated institution. His peaceful goal was, in his words, "the gradual, though total, abolition of slavery in the United States."

When Lundy came to Boston to find support for his cause, he quickly made a convert of Garrison. In 1829 the young man became the editor of Lundy's paper, *The Genius of Emancipation*. Once Garrison joined any cause, he applied himself to it heart and soul. Being thoroughly convinced of the wickedness of slavery, he dropped the idea of gradual abolition and came out boldly for immediate freedom. The peace-loving Lundy was becoming very uneasy, for these ardent reformers had bravely (or imprudently?) decided to publish their antislavery paper in Baltimore.

Located in a border state, Baltimore was a center of the domestic slave-shipping trade and full of slavery backers. Soon Garrison's forthright language was infuriating the slavery men and driving away the antislavery people. Threats of a beating—or worse—never scared Garrison. He merely replied forcefully that "slavery is a monster and must be treated as such."

When Garrison described the men who transported slaves as "highway robbers and murderers," he was promptly brought into court and fined fifty dollars. Garrison did not have the money; but even if he had had it, he would still have refused to pay. So he went to jail; after seven weeks of imprisonment, a wealthy abolitionist paid his fine and thus obtained his freedom.

Soon he lost a second suit and had to run away from Baltimore. It was one of the few times in his life that Garrison admitted that strategic retreat was the better part of valor.

But Lundy was alarmed at his young associate's outspokenness. The two men parted on unfriendly terms, and Garrison went off to Washington to found the *Public Liberator and Journal of the Times*. But the paper found no following. Public speaking and direct contact, Garrison decided, would make more converts to his cause.

Here too he ran into a snag; for, although he was a pious Baptist, many churches refused to let him speak. Nevertheless, Garrison persevered, and his speeches in Boston secured valuable allies. This encouraged him to move his paper to Boston, despite the strong proslavery sentiment in many parts of New England—particularly Boston—at that time.

Garrison was not discouraged by the sluggish or downright hostile reception he often experienced; he realized that the trend of the times favored him in some ways. Change was in the air. Thoughtful men and women saw the need for reform and were not afraid of it. Ralph Waldo Emerson boldly attacked outworn creeds, and his friend Henry Thoreau poured scorn on the routine thoughtlessness of his fellow men.

The promise of the Declaration of Independence and the French Revolution had not been fulfilled. Powerful reform movements originating in Europe were making their influence felt in the New World. A substantial number of clergymen wanted to see Christianity extended into everyday life, instead of being reserved for long Sunday sermons. Each religious group was in a state of civil war, with one faction stubbornly wedded to things as they were, and another faction just as eager for things as they should be. In national politics, the aim of Jacksonian Democracy was—to borrow a twentieth-century phrase—to introduce the century of the common man.

The 1830's were an exciting time in which to live. Horace Mann was beginning his lifelong task of drastically improving American schools. Working people were dissatisfied with long hours, poor conditions, low pay, lack of organization. The absurd injustice of the debtors' imprisonment laws cried for a humane solution. New religious sects, striving for a Christian approach to the problems of the day, were constantly coming into existence.

After enduring age-long discrimination, women were seeking equality before the law. The heartless methods of caring for the disabled, the poor, the aged, and the insane were gradually being reformed. The temperance movement was struggling to rescue the victims of heavy drinking. Utopian communities like Brook Farm, impractical but based on warmly generous impulses, strove to show men a more rewarding way of life.

Garrison shrewdly realized that the long pull was in his favor, despite the widespread opposition that he encountered. The antislavery movement was logically a part of the greater reform movement of the day. Its ethical unselfishness made it attractive to idealists, for men like Garrison risked martyrdom and had nothing to gain in a material sense from fighting to free the Negro. Sooner or later it would become clear to a majority of Americans that the existence of Negro slavery was a menace to the rights of the whole population.

This was far from clear to most Americans at the time that Garrison began his work. But, as the antislavery movement spread and as opposition to it hardened, fundamental American rights became shaky. Freedom of speech and the press were violated openly; freedom of assembly was menaced by "lynch law." Teachers, public speakers, and clergymen had to fight for the right to be heard. The right to use the mails was at the mercy of officials who took the law into their own hands, confiscating magazines that contained antislavery material. And so, over the years, the struggle over the abolitionist movement turned into a larger struggle over the very existence of the American form of government. The time was to come, as Abraham Lincoln eventually summed up the dilemma, when the United States could no longer exist half-slave and half-free.

In 1831 Garrison started a new paper, *The Liberator*, with these stirring words:

"I will be as harsh as truth and as uncompromising as justice. On this subject I do not wish to speak or write with moderation. I am in earnest, I will not equivocate; I will not excuse; I will not retreat a single inch—*and I will be heard*."

But for a time the world remained deaf to Garrison's trumpet blasts. He had six subscriptions during the first year, and only reached fifty-three the following year. The subscriptions increased slowly over the years, but Garrison kept the paper going until slavery was no longer the law of the land.

Nor did he ever miss an opportunity to be "heard." Once, when he was asked to tone down his harsh attacks on slavery, he replied, "My language is exactly such as suits me; it will displease many, I know—to displease them is my intention."

The existence of slavery in the District of Columbia made a perfect target for his stinging barbs: "We are ashamed when we know that the manacled slave is driven to market by the very doors of our Capitol, and sold like a beast in the very place where are assembled the representatives of a free and Christian people." Even in the North, people who did not relish such plain talk scoffed at him as "Lloyd Garrulous."

When a state legislature made it a crime to teach Negroes to read and write, Garrison was outraged: "There is something unspeakably pitiable and alarming in the state of that society where it is deemed necessary, for self-preservation, to seal up the mind and debase the intellect of man to brutal incapacity." These words are even more applicable to our own time.

Garrison has often been criticized for being unreasonable, but only an "extremist" would have continued to work in the face of the handicaps which beset him. In fact, a "reasonable" man would never have undertaken such a discouraging, disagreeable, potentially dangerous task in the first place. True, he was inflexible, but inflexibility was a virtue in the kind of struggle he had to wage. "There shall be no neutrals," he replied sternly when he was reproached. "Men shall either like me or dislike me."

Difficulties meant nothing to Garrison. In 1832 he organized the New England Anti-Slavery Society, set up an office in Boston, tirelessly gave lectures throughout New England, and slowly added to his slim list of subscribers. The South denounced him, and three Southern states set a price on his head; Garrison was flattered at this reluctant tribute.

In 1833 the abolition of slavery throughout the British Empire encouraged Garrison to take a leading part in forming the American Anti-Slavery Society. His crusade was now established on a nationwide basis. By this time his *Liberator* had 1400 subscribers, but he was still far from able to meet its expenses; from time to time enthusiastic supporters bailed him out.

Still Garrison refused to moderate the tone of the paper, and thus alienated people who were sympathetic to his views on slavery. Emerson commented tersely that *"The Liberator* is a scold." A distinguished minister remarked that Garrison did not "go to work like a Christian gentleman." Garrison was unmoved. He merely replied that "if those who deserve the lash feel it and wince at it, I shall be assured that I am striking the right person in the right place."

When Garrison organized the New England Anti-Slavery Society in 1832, it had 15 members. By 1840 the American Anti-Slavery Society had 2000 chapters with 250,000 members. Two events had a great deal to do with the growth of the organization. One was the assassination of Elijah Lovejoy and the other was the attempted murder of Garrison himself.

One evening in 1835 the opposition to Garrison took an ugly turn. A Boston mob of over a thousand men gathered near his office, seized him, and put a rope around him to hang him. Undoubtedly they would have carried out their intention if the Mayor had not intervened, rescued him from the mob, and put him in prison for safekeeping. It was on this occasion that Garrison scribbled these words on the wall of his prison cell:

"WLG was put into this cell on Wednesday afternoon, October 21, 1835, to save him from the violence of a respectable and influential mob, who sought to destroy him for preaching the abominable and dangerous doctrine that all men are created equal and that all oppression is odious in the sight of God. Confine me as a prisoner, but bind me not as a slave. Punish me as a criminal, but hold me not as a chattel. Torture me as a man, but drive me not like a beast. Doubt my sanity, but acknowledge my immortality."

Such was Garrison's reputation as a firebrand that people were astonished when they met him for the first time. He was a mild-mannered man of middle height, with hazel eyes and a ruddy complexion and had become bald in his twenties. In his family life he was a model husband and father, noted in this affectionate atmosphere for his gentle manners and quiet speech. In 1834 Garrison had married Helen Benson, the daughter of a retired merchant who lived in Roxbury. They had seven children, two of whom died in infancy.

In Garrison's old age he was visited by William H. Herndon, once Lincoln's law partner. Herndon was agreeably surprised. Expecting to find a crusty, harsh old man, he "found him warm, generous, approachable, communicative; he has some mirth, some wit, and a deep abiding faith in coming universal charity."

After being freed from prison, even Garrison realized that he had better leave Boston for a while, until passions had simmered down. Some newspapers held him responsible for the ugly incident. The *Transcript,* for example, saw deliberate provocation in his "rancorous denunciations, and his brawling, ferocious abuse."

The murder of Lovejoy had much wider repercussions. Elijah P. Lovejoy was a Presbyterian minister who edited a religious paper in which he took a strong abolitionist stand. After being driven from his home in St. Louis in 1837 because of his antislavery stand, he moved to Alton, Illinois. In short order his press was destroyed by a proslavery mob; he bought a new press, which was likewise destroyed; and a third press met the same fate.

With notable but unassuming courage, Lovejoy prepared to buy a fourth press. Peace-loving citizens begged him to flee for his life, but he refused.

"Why should I retreat again?" he asked in a moving speech. "When can I be safe again, if not here? Have not I a right to claim the protection of the laws? What more can I have in any other place? Sir, the very act of retreating will embolden the mob to follow me wherever I go: No sir, the contest has commenced here; and here it must be finished. Before God and you all, I here pledge myself to continue it, if need be till death. If I fall, my grave shall be made here in Alton."

When Lovejoy heroically resisted a lawless attempt to destroy his fourth press, he was shot and killed by an unknown assassin. This wanton murder rocked the whole nation with horror. Many Americans who had been indifferent to abolition arguments were at last won over to the antislavery cause. The martyrdom of Lovejoy dramatized the struggle against slavery more powerfully than any argument or editorial could have done.

For a long time Garrison opposed any political action on behalf of the Negro. He took the strange attitude that the Constitution was an accursed instrument and no good could come of it. The outcome was a bitter split in the abolitionist ranks between Garrison's followers and those who believed in gaining political power in order to remove a great evil by constitutional means.

The Compromise of 1850 was so disappointing to opponents of slavery that for a while Garrison's intransigent attitude seemed justified. The chief features of this law were:

California, which would never have any practical use for slave labor in any event, was to be admitted to the Union as a free state. The new territories won as a result of the Mexican War were all to be formed into slave states. Worse yet, there was a provision—the Fugitive Slave Law—that vastly increased the Federal government's powers in pursuing and seizing runaway slaves in free territory and forcibly returning them to their masters. Anyone helping the wretched fugitives was to be prosecuted as a criminal.

These last provisions enraged even those who were still lukewarm about slavery. As for Garrison, he surpassed himself in his attacks on Daniel Webster, who had put through the compromise in Congress in the hope of obtaining Southern support for the next Presidential campaign. Garrison described Webster's advocacy as "villainy of an unmitigated type, treachery to the cause of liberty and humanity of the blackest shade."

Despite the headlong violence of his words, Garrison came to believe firmly in nonresistance. He opposed all efforts to free the slaves by force. And so he could not approve of John Brown's fanatical attempt to start a slave revolt in Virginia in 1859 by trying to seize the arsenal at Harpers Ferry. These two men shared the same objective—emancipation—but they differed sharply on the means of achieving their aims.

Though Brown's attempted rebellion had to fail, it indicated to Garrison that the tension over slavery had almost reached the breaking point. "In firing his gun, John Brown has merely told us what time of day it is. It is high noon, thank God." The long-dreaded Civil War, which would come close to tearing the Union apart, was almost at hand.

It is interesting to compare Garrison's attitude toward slavery with Abraham Lincoln's views on the same subject. Lincoln hated slavery just as much as Garrison did, yet he felt—in 1837 at any rate, twenty-four years before the outbreak of the Civil War—that the preaching of the abolitionists "tends rather to increase than to abate" the evils of slavery.

Where Garrison was harsh, Lincoln was tolerant. Garrison saw a clean-cut struggle between good and evil; Lincoln realized that he lived in an imperfect world of imperfect people. Garrison concentrated on the evils of the present; Lincoln looked ahead to the problems of the future.

Garrison was an idealist who wanted morality to triumph; Lincoln, on the other hand, was prepared to sacrifice a great deal to preserve the Union. Garrison was a propagandist for what was ethically right; Lincoln was a practical statesman who was reconciled to compromising with evil—at least up to a point.

And yet, despite the profound differences between the two men, Lincoln in the end had to travel along the path marked out by Garrison. For all his lofty idealism, Garrison was not afraid to have force applied to bring about emancipation. For all his benevolent wisdom, Lincoln had to admit that some evils are so corrosive that only force can curb them.

When Lincoln first appeared on the national political scene, Garrison, in his usual "all-or-nothing" mood, heaped contempt and abuse on him. He was one of those Easterners who saw in Lincoln nothing but a country bumpkin. Yet once the war started, Garrison readily admitted that he had underestimated Lincoln; his ridicule changed to admiration, and while he stubbornly clung to his principles of nonresistance, he backed the North's attempt to stamp out secession.

Sentiment and logic must have struggled for a long time in Garrison's mind. He loathed violence, and yet if the South were to have its way, slavery would flourish more than ever. So Garrison supported the war, at the same time stoutly insisting that he was still a pacifist. His reasoning was impressive, but it did not change the fact that he had shifted his position.

Still, Garrison reserved the right to criticize; and Lincoln's caution in moving against slavery aroused his bitterest reproaches in private. The President, Garrison once remarked to a friend, "has evidently not a drop of anti-slavery blood in his veins, and he seems incapable of uttering a humane or generous sentiment respecting the enslaved millions in our land."

Yet as time went on, Garrison became more and more convinced of Lincoln's greatness; his subsequent criticisms were respectful in tone, reasonable in argument, and filled with sympathetic understanding of Lincoln's practical problems. Garrison's patience was rewarded when the Emancipation Proclamation became law on January 1, 1863. His struggle of more than thirty years' duration had been completed—victoriously.

In the old days, he had been called "incendiary" and "fanatic" and worse. Now other abolitionists who considered him too tame applied such epithets as "meek" and "conservative." In other words, Garrison, in his uncompromising way, had achieved the kind of worldly success which is supposed to be beyond the reach of idealists.

At the end of 1865, *The Liberator* appeared for the last time, bringing the news of the ratification of the Thirteenth Amendment. Hundreds of thousands of young men had given their lives before its brief text could come into existence:

"Neither slavery nor involuntary servitude, except as a punishment for crime, whereof the party shall have been duly convicted, shall exist within the United States, or any place subject to their jurisdiction."

In public life, Garrison displayed no humor and no feeling for gracious amenities. He judged everything in terms of right or wrong. There was no middle ground, no compromise. He was as stern and self-righteous as any Puritan. This frame of mind has often, in the history of mankind, led to abuses; but it has also given men the strength to right terrible wrongs. Garrison's great achievement was that in one of America's most critical periods, he was his country's conscience.

HENRY DAVID THOREAU

I learned this at least by my experiment, that if one advances confidently in the direction of his dreams, and endeavours to live the life which he has imagined, he will meet with a success unexpected in common hours. In proportion as he simplifies his life the laws of the Universe will appear less complex, and solitude will not be solitude, nor poverty poverty, nor weakness weakness.

Of the thirty-nine volumes that Thoreau wrote, only two were published during his lifetime. They were so far off the beaten track that both had to be published at his own expense. Neither book made money; in fact, one of them, *A Week on the Concord and Merrimack Rivers,* sold a mere 115 copies in four years, after which the publisher returned the remaining copies as unsalable. This lack of worldly success did not disturb Thoreau, for worldly success was the last thing that he sought or prized. "Those authors are successful," he observed, "who do not write to others, but make their own taste and judgment their audience." And he added: "It is enough if I please myself with writing; I am then sure of an audience."

Nor was his confidence misplaced, for in the century that has elapsed since his death, his *Walden* has come to be acknowledged as one of the greatest works of American literature. And, as the years pass and modern life becomes more routine and mechanized, the appeal of *Walden* continues to grow steadily.

Thoreau was a fierce and uncompromising individualist. "I desire that there may be as many different persons in the world as possible," he said. "But I would have each one be very careful to find out and pursue *his own way* and not his father's or his mother's or his neighbor's instead."

Like his friend Emerson, Thoreau stressed that each man's life must have quality, zest, savor. Just as Emerson noted that "we are always getting ready to live, but never living," so Thoreau asserted that he wished "to have my immortality now, in the quality of my daily living." His ambition was "to live deep and suck out all the marrow of life."

Again and again he returns to this theme: "We want no completeness but intensity of life." Impatient of shams, he expressed this thought even more ruthlessly when he wrote, "Be it life or death, we crave only reality. If we are really dying, let us hear the rattle in our throats and feel cold in the extremities; if we are alive, let us go about our business."

To achieve this intensity, Thoreau realized very quickly, it was necessary to live simply. His three basic principles were, "Simplicity, simplicity, simplicity!" To make his point clear, he added, "I say, let your affairs be as two or three, and not a hundred or a thousand;

instead of a million count half a dozen, and keep your accounts on your thumb-nail."

Thoreau despised wealth and the search for it. "In my experience," he said, "I have found nothing so impoverishing as what is called wealth." For, he shrewdly points out, as people become more prosperous, they "inevitably acquire a more expensive habit of living, and even the very same comforts and necessaries cost you more than they once did." A worrisome state of affairs, he concludes, and how pointless! For well-off people are prone to worry about a decrease in their income, although they might still be left with a sum that once would have assured them of comfort and ease.

How then should one earn a living? Farming? Shopkeeping? A trade? A profession? Thoreau finds them all hateful. Thoreau's aim in life was to devote almost all his time to what most people consider leisure. He studied trees and plants by the hour; he observed the creatures of forest and pond with fascination and a keenness that few men have attained; he studied oriental philosophy and Greek and Latin classics and related what he had read to what he had seen; he spent much of the remaining time recording his observations and reflections in the detailed journals from which his books were eventually fashioned. Although he lived in Concord all his life, he let his thought range over all eternity and over the entire universe. He found it worth his while to study an ant fight for several hours, instead of wasting his time working.

Thoreau was lucky to be living in Concord a century ago, where there was "mile after mile of embowered walks, such as no nobleman's grounds can boast, with animals running free and wild therein as from the first, —varied with land and water prospect, and above all, so retired that it is extremely rare that I meet a single wanderer in its mazes."

On his solitary walks Thoreau could watch the flight of geese or study the patterns of a leaf. Nearby were forests of pine, maple, spruce, and cedar. There were no filling stations, trailer-camp sites, soda-pop dispensing machines, or souvenir stands to mar his view. The day was still far in the future when the roar of motorboat engines would disturb the peaceful stillness of Walden Pond.

To obtain all these riches—and in Thoreau's eyes they were truly riches—he calculated that he had to work no more than forty days a year. He worked at odd times for the little money he needed—as a surveyor, handy man, or in the family pencil factory. He was a skilled carpenter and loved to work with his hands—but for the pleasure of it rather than for money. He also augmented his income by occasionally giving lectures.

Thoreau was born on July 12, 1817; thus he was Emerson's junior by some fourteen years. Thoreau's mother kept a boardinghouse, and it is very likely that the constant presence of a great many people in his home strongly influenced his fondness for solitude.

He had a large tribe of aunts and uncles, all of them strongly marked personalities. Though the Thoreaus had an affectionate relationship, his mother had such a dominating personality that this too would help ex-

plain young Thoreau's desire for solitude and independence. Yet he enjoyed returning to the family circle
from time to time.

There was a close bond between Henry and his elder
brother John, who was his companion on the memorable
trip later described in *A Week on the Concord and
Merrimack Rivers.* John's early death had a depressing
effect on Henry which lasted for years.

As a child Henry was quiet and well behaved, given
to daydreaming and so self-possessed that he was nicknamed "the Judge." He received a good education at
the Concord Academy, where he studied Latin, Greek,
and French. It was here too that he learned to play the
flute, which became one of his greatest pleasures in
later life.

If we are to judge from a passage in *Walden,* his
taste for the outdoors was already keenly developed in
childhood:

"I have spent many an hour, when I was younger,
floating over its surface as the zephyr willed, having
paddled my boat to the middle, and lying on my back
across the seats, in a summer forenoon, dreaming awake,
until I was aroused by the boat touching the sand, and
I arose to see what shore my fates had impelled me to;
days when idleness was the most attractive and pro-
ductive industry. Many a forenoon have I stolen away,
preferring to spend thus the most valued part of the
day; for I was rich, if not in money, in sunny hours
and summer days, and spent them lavishly; nor do I
regret that I did not waste more of them in the work-
shop or the teacher's desk."

Thoreau attended Harvard College as a scholarship student but did not rank very high in his class because of illness and absence. Neither then nor later did he think much of his college education; a college, he said, dealt with branches of knowledge—"all the branches and none of the roots."

He must have been an extremely shy young man. John Weiss, a classmate, described him as cold and reserved. He generally kept his eyes fixed on the ground, even during a conversation, and he reminded Weiss of "some Egyptian sculpture of faces, large-featured but brooding, immobile, fixed in a mystic egoism." The only course for which he showed genuine enthusiasm was English literature; he read the poets from Chaucer to the Elizabethans with complete absorption.

But on the whole there are few signs of the mature Thoreau in his college years. One of them came in his Commencement speech, when he dropped this bombshell: "The order of things should be somewhat reversed; the seventh should be man's day of toil, wherein to earn his living by the sweat of his brow; and the other six his Sabbath of the affections and the soul,—in which to range this widespread garden, and drink in the soft influences and sublime reverences of Nature."

When Thoreau's college days were over, he had difficulty deciding what to do for a living. He had no intention of devoting his life to mere drudgery or making money. Finally he settled on teaching, although this was only a stopgap. When he started teaching, he announced that he would not beat the pupils. After only two weeks he was reprimanded by the head of the school, as a refusal to flog was virtually unheard of in those days. To show his contempt for what he considered a stupid and unjust custom, he beat six children at random with a ruler, and then resigned.

After futile attempts to get another teaching job, Henry opened a school in Concord with his brother John in 1838. Both young men had a way with children. The students flourished in the kindly, affectionate atmosphere. Despite the astonishment of outsiders, there was no need for flogging or even for lectures on good behavior. The weekly nature study trips in the woods were a special treat. The children picked flowers, watched the birds, looked for arrowheads, and even tried their hand at surveying. It seemed that Henry had at last found his niche, but these happy times came to a sudden end when John died at a very young age in 1841.

The school closed, and at twenty-four young Thoreau again faced the problem of how to live worthily and how to earn a living without succumbing to drudgery and routine. His needs were simple and few, and for several years he worked for Emerson, taking care of his garden, doing all necessary repairs, acting as companion for the Emerson children, and in general making himself useful.

Thoreau had started visiting Emerson in 1838. Emerson recorded this comment in his journal: "I delight much in my young friend, who seems to have as free and erect a mind as any I have ever met." On these visits Thoreau met some of the most distinguished intellectuals of the age. For the first time in his life he was stimulated by far-ranging ideas, good conversation, and a depth of learning that related the sages and prophets of olden times to the problems of his own time. Each meeting was like a game of ping-pong with fresh concepts.

In company he was still somewhat shy and easily provoked. One observer describes him as sitting "with a certain iron-pokerish-ness." Oliver Wendell Holmes commented that Thoreau "insisted on nibbling his asparagus at the wrong end." Emerson noted, good-humoredly but with a trace of exasperation, that "Henry does not feel himself except in opposition. He wants a fallacy to expose, a blunder to pillory, requires a little sense of victory, a roll of the drums, to call his powers into full exercise." A neighbor was doubtless thinking of the same quality when she said she could love Thoreau, but could not like him.

Thoreau's obvious superiority lay at the root of his trouble. As Emerson realized, Thoreau "understood the matter at a glance, and saw the limitations and poverty of those he had talked with, so that nothing seemed concealed from such terrible eyes." But Emerson had to admit wryly that "Henry is—with difficulty— sweet."

In later years the two men went through periods of estrangement. In their earlier years their mutual likes and interests were most prominent; as they grew older, their divergences became more pronounced.

In any event, Thoreau was honest to the point of oc- casional brusqueness, and his unconventional ways were not to everyone's taste. He was not blind to this side of his personality, and when an admirer wrote requesting a meeting, he replied: "You may rely on it that you have the best of me in my books, and that I am not worth seeing personally, the stuttering, blundering clodhopper that I am."

A petty man would not have been this blunt about himself. On the other hand, such frankness is usually wasted, as the recipient of such remarks takes them as a joke.

At any rate, given Thoreau's taste for solitude, his decision to live alone for some time was a perfectly logical one. He spent two years in the little house he built for himself on the shores of Walden Pond and, if we are to believe his famous account of his life there, he enjoyed every moment.

There is a popular but mistaken impression that Thoreau lived a hermit-like existence during this time. When he wanted company he went into Concord, occasionally gave lectures, received visits from friends, and at one point went off to the Maine woods.

Other misconceptions about Thoreau's life at Walden have arisen because his friends interpreted his purpose in terms of their own temperaments. Joseph Hosmer, himself a humdrum realist, described Thoreau as "one of the most practical of men, but without imagination or fancy, and what was not real was unworthy of his thought."

On the other hand, Bronson Alcott, whose head was always in the clouds, ecstatically described Thoreau as a "wood-nymph" and "the ruddiest and nimblest genius that has trodden our woods," living "amidst mists and exhalations." The fact is that Thoreau cannot be reduced to a formula. His character had both of these qualities, and each man saw only what his own character would qualify him to perceive.

There was hard realism and yet extraordinary insight in Thoreau's demonstration that "the student who wishes for a shelter can obtain one for a lifetime at an expense not greater than the rent which he now pays annually." Again, Thoreau was both hardheaded and subtle when he pointed out that it was easy to realize the grossly obvious exploitation of Negro slavery, but much more difficult to admit to oneself that the supposedly free man was a slave to many unseen masters. From such masters—social pressures, competitive display, absorption in routine work, Thoreau meant to be free, and thus to set an example to his fellow men.

Most men would be astounded to learn from Thoreau that the purpose of man's life is to "glorify God and enjoy him forever" rather than to crawl "down the road of life, pushing a barn and one hundred acres of land, tillage, mowing, pasture, and woodlot." Translate this into modern terms and the essentially unrewarding aspects of contemporary life, and we can understand Thoreau's scornful comment: "It is a fool's life, as they will find when they get to the end of it, if not before."

What then did Thoreau seek in living by himself? It is best to let him speak for himself, as he does in *Walden*, devoting the first eighty pages or so to explaining the reasons that brought him there and telling us what he learned from his experience.

First he slyly apologizes for talking so much about himself: "I should not talk so much about myself if there were anybody else whom I knew as well." Then, by an easy transition, Thoreau is soon turning the ordinary man's world upside down. Conventional people wonder how he obtained food, whether he was afraid to live alone, whether the feeling of being so different from other people did not bother him.

Thoreau retaliates good-humoredly by saying that his fellow townsmen remind him of religious cults in India which specialize in voluntary penance, such as hanging head downward over flames, or looking at the heavens over their shoulders for so long that they can no longer resume the natural position of the body.

If anything, he adds, doubtless with a twinkle in his eye, the citizens of Concord torture themselves even more painfully and pointlessly. Having inherited or acquired "farms, houses, barns, cattle, farming tools," they toil unceasingly by the sweat of their brows, with never a moment for reflection, for enjoying the beauty of nature, for creative interests. The workingman "has no time to be anything but a machine."

And why bother to keep up with the Joneses? Comfortable old clothes are all a man needs. After all, "We know but few men, a great many coats and breeches." For Thoreau, the familiar adage that "clothes make the man" has little point. And so he warns us: "Beware of all enterprises that require new clothes, and not rather a new wearer of clothes."

Fashion fares no better at Thoreau's hands. "The head monkey at Paris puts on a traveller's cap, and all the monkeys in America do the same." One notable sentence brilliantly lights up the serious purpose of his assault on fashion: "When the soldier is hit by a cannon-ball, rags are as becoming as purple." In other words, when we come to the decisive events of a lifetime, elegance and fashion are reduced to their true unimportance.

Thoreau is equally unimpressed by the civilized man's housing requirements. Shelter, as he sees it, is merely one's outermost garment. The Indian is quite snug and comfortable in a wigwam which can be put together or dismantled in a day; the white man, who is supposed to be so much further advanced in the arts of living, dwells in a house that has to be paid for with years of work. Who is the wiser man?

But now Thoreau, who has the conventionally thinking reader at his mercy, presses the argument further: The Indian owns his wigwam, whereas the white man very often has to pay rent to a landlord—he does not even own the shelter which takes away so much of his income. Is it so clear then, Thoreau inquires mockingly, that the white man is richer in any real sense than the Indian?

And so Thoreau says, in a phrase that Emerson used effectively later, it is not clear whether the farmer has a house or whether the house has the farmer. When the farmer cannot dispose of it because of some structural defect, he adds, only death can set the owner free.

And then what of the "silent poor"—those whose poverty more than balances the luxuries of the rich? What about those who live in miserable huts no better than pigsties; what of the wretched shanties near the railroad tracks? Is it not ironic, Thoreau asks, that a North American Indian or South Sea Islander has better shelter than a British workman or an Irish peasant?

When Thoreau was ready to build his own house, he borrowed an ax instead of buying one, on the theory that it was more generous to let someone else have an interest in the enterprise. "The owner, as he released his hold on it, said that it was the apple of his eye; but I returned it sharper than I received it." On his trips to the pine forest he took along a lunch of bread and butter wrapped in a newspaper which he read while he ate. For $4.25 he bought a ramshackle shanty and took it apart for nails, planks, and other parts. As Thoreau worked at a leisurely pace, several months passed before the house was framed and roofed.

The solid construction of his house protected him from rain, and he now proceeded with a carefully built chimney, so that he would be snugly shielded against the harsh New England winter. At this stage he had little time for reading, but he assures us that the stray scraps of paper he came across from time to time were as entertaining as the *Iliad*.

The house was fifteen by ten feet. It had two large windows, two trapdoors, and a brick fireplace. The total cost, not counting the value of his labor, came to $28.12½. (In those days the United States still had a half-cent coin.) In terms of present-day values, this might be figured as equivalent to about $125.

So, using the simplest means, Thoreau had obtained

just what he wanted. Means, methods, inventions, techniques are all very well; but in thinking of our means we can easily forget about our purposes, our objectives. So, as Thoreau asks, why expend a great deal of effort doing things that may not be worth doing?

"We are in great haste to construct a magnetic telegraph from Maine to Texas; but Maine and Texas, it may be, have nothing important to communicate." (More than a century has passed since Thoreau wondered about this, and his skeptical attitude is still in order.) "Either is in such a predicament as the man who was earnest to be introduced to a distinguished deaf woman, but when he was presented, and one end of her trumpet was put into his hand, had nothing to say. As if the main object were to talk fast and not to talk sensibly."

Thoreau had little patience with people who devote most of their lives to working very hard in order to acquire useless luxuries. "This spending of the best part of one's life earning money in order to enjoy a questionable liberty during the least valuable part of it reminds me of the Englishman who went to India to make a fortune first, in order that he might return to England and live the life of a poet. He should have gone up garret at once."

Thoreau's living expenses were trifling, as he planted two acres of beans, potatoes, corn, peas, and turnips. His eating tastes were so simple that his food purchases for a period of eight months came to $8.74, including twenty-two cents for pork—the only meat item on the list. He concluded that he could get along on eight dollars a month all told, a cheap enough price for "leisure, independence and health thus secured," as well as a "comfortable house for me as long as I choose to occupy it."

Thoreau took pride in baking his own bread, but this can hardly be taken as a sign of Spartan simplicity; he spent so much time on experimentation and research on methods and recipes—going back even to Roman times—that his preoccupation with the subject seems just as silly as the obsession with luxuries that he loves to ridicule.

To satisfy his needs for furniture was easy, for Thoreau held that "the more you have of such things the poorer you are." To show that the point is well taken, he mentions the recent auction sale of a deacon's effects which included a dried tapeworm. This passion for saving useless trifles does not seem out of place in a region where people are said to save bits of string and to keep a special box for bits of string that are too small to save.

As we have seen, Thoreau found that forty days of work a year were ample to supply all his material needs; the remainder of the year he could spend as he pleased. "In short," he concludes, "I am convinced, both by faith and experience, that to maintain oneself on this earth is not a hardship, but a pastime, if we will live simply and wisely. . . . It is not necessary that a man should earn his living by the sweat of his brow, unless he sweats easier than I do."

Out of the rich contentment of his contemplative

life at Walden, he asks, "Why should we live with such hurry and waste of life?" (What would he say if he were living in our time?) "Men say a stitch in time saves nine, and so they take a thousand stitches to-day to save nine to-morrow."

Although Thoreau's nearest neighbor was a mile away, Thoreau had all the company he needed:

"As I sit at my window this summer afternoon, hawks are circling about my clearing; the tantivy of wild pigeons, flying by twos and threes athwart my view, or perching restless on the white pine boughs behind my house, gives a voice to the air; a fish hawk dimples the glassy surface of the pond and brings up a fish; a mink steals out of the marsh before my door and seizes a frog by the shore; the sedge is bending under the weight of the reed-birds flitting hither and thither; and for the last half-hour I have heard the rattle of railroad cars, now dying away and then reviving like the beat of a partridge."

Some of the most enchanting passages in *Walden* are those in which Thoreau tells us how much he savors the peace of solitude—passages like this one: "Some of my pleasantest hours were during the long rainstorms in the spring or fall, which confined me to the house for the afternoon as well as the forenoon, soothed by their ceaseless roar and pelting; when an early twilight ushered in a long evening in which many thoughts had time to take root and unfold themselves."

This kind of solitude was pleasant; but there are other kinds that are painful—when people live close

together in towns, for example, and have nothing to
say to each other. "We are for the most part more lonely
when we go abroad among men than when we stay in
our chambers." What is etiquette, he asks, but a set of
rules for making the boredom of society more toler-
able?

Going along in this paradoxical vein, Thoreau continues in a famous passage, "I have a great deal of
company in my house, especially in the morning, when
nobody calls." If he wanted conversation, now and then,
the need was easily remedied. "Every day or two I
strolled to the village to hear some of the gossip which
is incessantly going on there, circulating either from
mouth to mouth, or from newspaper to newspaper."
Taken in small doses, this gossip "is really as refreshing
in its way as the rustle of leaves and the peeping of frogs."

But it was always good to get home again—"it is
not worth the while to go round the world to count
the cats in Zanzibar." And to keep up with the times
by reading a newspaper meant little to Thoreau.
Another murder, another fatal accident, another fire
—what did it matter? "One is enough. If you are
acquainted with the principle, what do you care for
a myriad instances and applications? To a philosopher
all *news*, as it is called, is gossip, and they who edit and
read it are old women over their tea."

But reading books—that was something else again.
Few men have written as eloquently as Thoreau about
the delight of great books to those who love them. "A
man, any man, will go considerably out of his way to
pick up a silver dollar; but here are golden words,

which the wisest men of antiquity have uttered, and whose worth the wise of every succeeding age have assured us of." Yet this treasure, which may be had for the taking, is rejected by most people: "Our reading, our conversation and thinking, are all on a very low level, worthy only of pygmies and manikins."

From reading, Thoreau passes on to education in general, and the passage of time has only underlined the force of his argument: "It is time that villages were universities, and their elder inhabitants the fellows of universities, with leisure—if they are, indeed, so well off—to pursue liberal studies the rest of their lives."

But why limit education to the young? So Thoreau advocates adult education, which in our own time has enrolled millions of students. Because Thoreau was ahead of his age in making this suggestion, it was scoffed at as another visionary idea. "What with foddering the cattle and tending the store, we are kept from school too long, and our education is sadly neglected." Thoreau has an even bolder idea which has not yet gained acceptance in our own time: much larger sums should be spent on education, that perennial Cinderella of public spending. "In this country, the village should in some respects take the place of the nobleman of Europe. It should be the patron of the fine arts. It is rich enough. It wants only the magnanimity and refinement."

Thoreau ridicules the notion that penny-pinching on education is true economy. The village "can spend enough on such things as farmers and traders value, but it is thought Utopian to propose spending money which more intelligent men know to be of far more worth. This town has spent seventeen thousand dollars on a town-house, thank fortune or politics, but probably it will not spend so much on living wit, the true meat to put into that shell, in a hundred years."

His conclusion is magnificent: "Instead of noblemen, let us have noble villages of men. If it is necessary, omit one bridge over the river, go round a little there, and throw one arch at least over the darker gulf of ignorance which surrounds us."

Eventually Thoreau decided to leave Walden and to return to the village: he "had several more lives to live, and could not spare any more time for that one." But he had achieved his main purpose. He had solitude when he wanted it, he read and reflected a great deal, and spent happy hours of intense absorption in the natural beauties of Walden. By living in the simplest possible manner, he proved his point—that it was possible to live enjoyably on next to nothing a year. Thoreau's friend William Ellery Channing said of his house that "it had no lock on the door, no curtains to the window, and belonged to nature nearly as much as man."

Channing has left us an unforgettable description of Thoreau at this time:

"The features were quite marked: the nose aquiline or very Roman; large, overhanging brows above the deepest-set blue eyes that could be seen, in certain lights, and in others gray—eyes expressive of all kinds of feeling, but never weak or nearsighted; the forehead not unusually broad or high, full of concentrated energy and purpose; the mouth with prominent lips, pursed

up with meaning and thought when silent, and giving
out when open a stream of the most varied and unusual
and instructive sayings.

"His hair was a dark brown, exceedingly abundant,
fine, and soft; and for several years he wore a comely
beard. His whole figure had an active earnestness, as
if he had no moment to waste. The clenched hand be-
tokened purpose. In walking, he made a short cut if he
could, and when sitting in the shade or by the wall-side,
seemed merely the clearer to look forward into the next
piece of activity. Even in the boat he had a wary,
transitory air, his eyes on the outlook—perhaps there
might be ducks, or the Blondin turtle, or an otter, or
sparrow."

Thoreau took a three-hour walk every day in the
fields or woods around Concord—or he might spend
some time on the river. He was always careful to take
along his spyglass and notebook. He would take quick,
basic notes and afterward write them up in considerable
but vivid detail in his journal. For necessary measure-
ments he took along a ruler and a surveyor's tape. He
noted the condition of plants, the appearance of animals,
the circumference of a tree trunk, or the depth of a
snowfall. On his way home he brought back plant
specimens, minerals, lichens, nuts—whatever was of special interest. He was always fascinated by the flight
of birds—hawks, thrushes, migrating warblers, and all
the rest.

The great theme that runs through Thoreau's writings is the conflict between society and the individual.
He saw that man was gaining ever greater mastery

over his environment, but was neglecting his spiritual development. Man was acquiring more power, but what was happening to the wisdom and insight that were needed to manage the new machines?

To give a simple example of this trend in our own day: we install more and more horsepower in our motor engines, but we give less thought to whether our drivers are safe and competent. Thus we entrust more and more power to drivers who are progressively more inadequately equipped to drive.

Sensitive people who have occupied themselves with this problem often come to the eerie conclusion that man himself is becoming enslaved to the machines he has devised. Hence Thoreau's famous observation: "We do not ride on the railroad; it rides upon us." Most people unthinkingly accept the domination of the mechanical monsters—but not Thoreau. "If the engine whistles, let it whistle till it is hoarse for its pains. If the bell rings, why should we run?"

Signs of the new age were multiplying around him even in the idyllic Concord area. Though the river banks were still in much the same state as in Indian days, his delightful boat excursions were marred by the sight of the debris floating down from a nearby factory. Yet such distressing portents could never curb Thoreau's rebellious spirit.

Thoreau distrusted the political state to such an extent that he never voted. But he discovered eventually that he could not ignore questions like the tariff or states' rights, and above all, Negro slavery. Very gradually he realized that in staying aloof from politics, he was contributing to the very conditions which he loathed.

The struggle in Thoreau's mind came to a head in 1846 over the annexation of Texas as a slave state. Thoreau felt he had to take a public stand against this act, if only to maintain his self-respect. Boldly he denounced a state of affairs that most Americans managed to ignore or explain away: "A sixth of the population of a nation which has undertaken to be the refuge of liberty are slaves."

Thoreau was no longer satisfied to withdraw and let history take its course. But the individual was helpless—or was he? So Thoreau refused to pay his poll tax; he declined to support a government which made slavery the law of the land. For this he was imprisoned in the Concord jail for one night, and released the next morning when an aunt paid the tax for him.

In later years Thoreau self-consciously wondered sometimes whether his gesture had been worthwhile. In such moments it seemed the ostentatious gesture of a crank—but basically it was the desperate attempt of one courageous individual to preserve his integrity.

From this experience Thoreau developed his doctrine of Civil Disobedience. But if every man were to decide whether he should obey the state or not, would not the result be chaos? After all, when the men of the South later decided that rebellion was preferable to the disappearance of slavery, were they not following Thoreau's example and applying his reasoning that justified resistance to the power of the state?

But Thoreau had foreseen such dilemmas and had

dealt with them in these wise words: "If the injustice
is part of the necessary friction of the machine of
government, let it go; perchance it will wear smooth.
But if it is of such a nature that it requires you to be the
agent of injustice to another, then, I say, break the law."

In his own time Thoreau's views on Civil Disobedience were ignored or ridiculed. Yet almost a century later Mahatma Gandhi achieved freedom for India
through passive resistance, and a few years later Kwame
Nkrumah successfully followed his example to win independence for the Gold Coast colony in Africa. More
recently the Negroes of Birmingham, Alabama, applied
the same tactics in a courageous boycott of segregated
bus travel.

In all these cases, the inspiration for resistance came,
directly or indirectly, from Thoreau's doctrine of Civil
Disobedience. No force was used, no violence was offered by the dissenters.

Unfortunately in the America of the 1850's, the
growing intensification of the bitter dispute over slavery
was heading toward a violent explosion. The Fugitive
Slave Act was just as obnoxious to Thoreau as it was
to Emerson. In a speech delivered in 1854, Thoreau
attacked this iniquitous law with all his formidable
powers of sarcasm and invective.

"If I were seriously to propose to Congress," he said,
"to make mankind into sausages, I have no doubt that
most of the members would smile at my proposition,
and if any believed me to be in earnest, they would
think that I proposed something much worse than
Congress had ever done. But if any of them will tell

me that to make a man into a sausage would be much
worse,—would be any worse,—than to make him into a
slave,—than it was to enact the Fugitive Slave Law,
—I will accuse him of foolishness, of intellectual incapacity, of making a distinction without a difference."

Five years later, when John Brown raided the Federal arsenal at Harpers Ferry, Virginia, in the hope of
starting a revolt to free the slaves, he was denounced
as a fanatic and a lunatic even by the abolitionists.
Thoreau was almost alone in defending Brown and in
praising him as a deeply ethical man moved by solely
humanitarian motives. He was particularly struck by
Brown's final words to the court after being sentenced
to hanging:

"I want you to understand that I respect the rights
of the poorest and weakest of colored people, oppressed
by the slave power, just as much as I do those of the
most wealthy and powerful.

"I wish to say, furthermore, that you had better, all
you people at the South, prepare yourselves for a settlement of that question, that must come up for settlement sooner than you are prepared for it. The sooner
you are prepared the better. You may dispose of me
very easily. I am nearly disposed of now; but this
question is still to be settled,—this negro question, I
mean; the end of that is not yet."

It took less than two years for John Brown's grim
prophecy to be fulfilled in the outbreak of the Civil
War. But in the meantime Thoreau was attacked by
the tuberculosis which had already carried off so many
members of his family. It would have given him great

joy to see the Emancipation Proclamation go into effect; but he died in 1862, before that came to pass.

We are told that Thoreau met death stoically and patiently, retaining his dry humor to the end. When his aunt asked him if he had made his peace with God, he replied, "I was not aware that we had ever quarreled." When another visitor began speaking about the possibility of an afterlife, he whispered feebly, "One world at a time."

Thoreau's life had a wholeness and straightforward development that is given to few human beings to achieve. He practiced what he preached; he lived as he wanted to; he attacked lies, shams, injustices, and the shabbiness of "the mass of men," who, he said memorably, "lead lives of quiet desperation."

Though he was a tireless seeker for truth, he was content with the realization that the quest could never end. "At the same time that we are earnest to explore and learn all things, we require that all things be mysterious and unexplorable, that land and sea be infinitely wild, unsurveyed by us because unfathomable." In the same way, Thoreau will continue to attract and inspire readers, without ever quite yielding up his ultimate secret.

OLIVER WENDELL HOLMES

Only when you have worked alone,—when you have felt around you a black gulf of solitude more isolating than that which surrounds the dying man, and in hope and despair have trusted to your own unshaken will,— then only will you have achieved.

Oliver Wendell Holmes has been called the greatest American of his time. This man who at the age of twenty-one was left for dead on the battlefield of Antietam, survived to live just six years short of a century.

When Holmes was born in 1841, there were twenty-seven states in the Union and William Henry Harrison had just been inaugurated President. At the time of Holmes's death in 1935, Franklin Delano Roosevelt was President and a quarter of a century had elapsed since the admission of the forty-eighth state. In the world into which he was born, railways and steamships were still something of a novelty, and the Morse telegraph had not yet been invented; old John Quincy Adams, getting up before dawn, was still lighting his fire with flint and steel. A century later, intensive research was being lavished on atomic fission, antibiotics, radar, super-bombers and other scientific marvels.

Just as sweeping was Justice Holmes's vista of the American scene. He was five years old at the outbreak of the Mexican War; as a youth he fought in some of the most terrible battles of the Civil War; and he died only four years before the outbreak of World War II. As an old man of eighty-three, steeped in memories of bygone times, he would recall that his grandmother had died in 1862, at a time when he was involved in some of the fiercest fighting of the Civil War; and he was reminded of the old woman's recollections of the occupation of Boston by the British at the beginning of the Revolutionary War. The Revolution still had personal meaning for him—it was not merely something one read about in books.

Holmes was an extraordinarily complex man. He cannot be pinned down in a few words or summed up in a single sentence. He was one of those rare men who become more handsome as they grow older; his erect stature, his drooping mustaches and deep-set, probing eyes directly conveyed an aristocratic nature which impressed everyone at first glance. "His conversation and bearing," one friend observed, "were like a rare music that lingers in one's memory." He was an aristocrat by temperament, a conservative by inclination; study and reflection made him a skeptic. He detested senti-mentality—"I have had thoughts," he wrote William James in 1907, "on the need of a society for the promotion of hard-heartedness."

Few men have understood the power of thought, and the need for it, as well as Holmes did. "To know," he said memorably, "is not less than to feel. A valid idea is worth a regiment any day." Like Thoreau before him, Holmes detested newspapers and never read them. Their pettiness, their vulgarity, their lack of reflectiveness, all repelled him.

Whether speaking or writing, Holmes expressed himself gracefully and wittily; sometimes he was ironic, sometimes deeply thoughtful, sometimes both. The characteristic mixture is seen in his remark as an old man that "probably I am too skeptical as to our ability to do more than shift disagreeable burdens from the shoulders of the stronger to those of the weaker."

And he added, "I believe that the wholesale social regeneration which so many now seem to expect, if it can be helped by conscious, co-ordinated human effort, cannot be effected appreciably by tinkering with the institution of property, but only by taking in hand life and trying to build a race."

Here he was echoing, no doubt intentionally, Emerson's doctrine that the world could be improved, not by this or that specific reform, but only by changing man's basic nature. Yet Holmes readily admitted that a young friend had made a convincing answer when he told the Justice that "you would base legislation upon regrets rather than hopes."

Again like Emerson and Thoreau, Holmes thought that the greatest good was to get the most out of life. As he put it with characteristic slyness: "On the whole I am on the side of the unregenerate who affirm the worth of life as an end in itself as against the saints who

deny it." Perhaps Holmes forever retained the psychol-
ogy of the combat soldier who is aware at all times that
each day may be his last. On another occasion he voiced
the same thought in this way, "Life is an end in itself,
and the only question as to whether it is worth living
is whether you have enough of it."

Unlike most skeptics, Holmes was urbane enough to
extend his skepticism to himself: "To have doubted
one's own first principles is the mark of a civilized man."
By this criterion, Holmes was indeed a civilized man,
for in his fifty years on the bench he was often tolerant
of the existence of doctrines that he despised. The doctrine of "live and let live" was best after all, for "my
neighbor is better nourished by eating his own dinner
than by my eating it for him."

It is curious that from these expressions of unbelief
there gradually emerges a pattern of belief. If life is
worth living, then it is desirable to act so that life will
be worth living. The stern Puritan ethic which
Holmes's ancestors had applied to religion he trans-
planted into his career in the law. And why not? "All
callings are great when greatly pursued." Here his
urbanity gives way to an intensity that few men have
matched: "The joy of life is to put forth one's power
in some natural or useful or harmless way. There is no
other." And: "Whatsoever thy hand findeth to do, do
it with all thy might."

Holmes's searing combat experiences in the Civil
War, instead of embittering him, reinforced the Puritan
influence. Recalling that more than half of his Harvard

ings were even more popular in England than in his native Boston, and his *Autocrat of the Breakfast-Table* was a favorite with every well-read Englishman.

The son was proud of his father's fame, yet oppressed by it as well. On his first visit to England someone asked him, "Are you the son of Dr. Holmes?" and he replied, "No, he is my father." Years later, when the son, now a man of over forty, was appointed to the Massachusetts Supreme Court, the father spoke at a public dinner and with every appearance of good nature managed to sweep away his son's satisfaction at the honor with this remark: "To *think* of it—my little boy a judge, and able to send me to jail if I don't behave myself." And he went on to recite a poem, specially prepared for the occasion, in which he alluded to the sight of baby food dribbling down his infant son's chin. In that way, perhaps, the father recaptured the superiority that had been his, forty years ago.

As the years passed the hostile feelings died down; and as the Justice grew older, he began to see his father in a more favorable light. The differences between the two men were caused by their conflict, which in turn widened the differences. But there was much for which the son was indebted to the father. It may well be that these two opposed influences account for the paradoxical qualities we have noticed in the younger Holmes.

In his desire to live greatly, to achieve something significant, to follow the unknown end, we see the son's yearning for independence. But the father's influence is seen in many Holmesian traits: his playful irony, his skepticism, the charm of his conversation, his conservatism, his admiration for British culture, his abiding love for his country, his mastery of the written and spoken word. Whatever conflicts were involved, his upbringing gave him the unusual advantage of inspiring contacts with some of the greatest men of the day. Thanks to his father's relations with the great and the near-great, the son made the acquaintance of distinguished writers, poets, philosophers, and scientists. These included Nathaniel Hawthorne, James Russell Lowell, Longfellow, Emerson, and two of the leading scientists of the period, Louis Agassiz and Asa Gray.

In the ambitious struggle between father and son the father came off second-best; for, while the son is remembered today for what he *did*, the father is remembered for what he *was*—the father of a famous man. Yet in his own day Holmes senior achieved lasting fame at the age of twenty-one with his stirring poem, *Old Ironsides*. In 1830 the frigate *U.S.S. Constitution* was to be scrapped. Furious at the destruction of the warship that had won such glorious victories in the War of 1812, Holmes wrote the poem ("Ay! pull her tattered ensign down!") that swept the country and made him famous overnight. The popular clamor created by the poem was so great that the government had to rescind its order; to this day the famous vessel, after innumerable repairs, may still be seen in Boston harbor.

But writing poetry was no way to make a living, so Holmes chose medicine as a profession that was both absorbing and the source of a passable income. At first the sufferings of hospital patients and the horrors of operations without anesthetics depressed him, but after a while he began to love his work and found it deeply satisfying.

He rounded out his medical studies with two and a half years in the Paris hospitals, where, as he said, he learned "not to take authority when I can have facts; not to guess when I can know." The son, many years later, was to apply the same attitude toward the law. In 1836 the elder Holmes received his M.D. from Harvard. But his love of literature had grown with the years. Holmes had a way with words, jokes, puns, witty phrases, and rollicking satire that made him a popular companion and after-dinner speaker. Building a medical practice was a discouragingly slow process, so Holmes took a part-time post as Professor of Anatomy at Dartmouth. Then, together with several partners, he founded a fairly successful medical school in Boston. In 1847 he was appointed Professor of Anatomy and Physiology at Harvard, where he became one of the most popular members of the faculty.

That Wendell would attend Harvard was always taken for granted. His scholastic achievement after his entry in 1857 was something less than sensational. In his freshman class he was twenty-second in a group of eighty. During the sophomore year he dropped to thirtieth. Just what the formal record proves is not clear, for in those days the Harvard grades were strongly affected by substantial demerits for such dread deeds as focusing sunlight in the Harvard Yard with a piece of glass. And we may recall that the college work of Emerson and Thoreau was equally mediocre.

Yet Wendell was far from idle. Judging from an essay he wrote at this time for the college magazine, he was doing a great deal of reading—not necessarily prescribed reading. "Read for ideas, not for authors," he advises his fellow students. "I cannot get beyond the belief that it is best to read what we like." This harmless-sounding statement is probably a thrust at the authorities who in that day and age told him that it is best to read what we *ought* to read, like it or not.

The young writer continues, "Those who have somewhat higher aspirations than the mass of their companions and who in the ranks of boyish insipidity do not find or meet their desires, must as an alternative turn to books." There is a hint here of loneliness, though he had plenty of friends. Already his tastes were forming along lines that set him apart from most of his fellows. During his junior year he continued to read intensively, but his grades improved.

Modesty struggled with pride when he contributed to the Class Autobiography. Toward the beginning he pointed out that "all my three names designate families from which I am descended," but he wound up with: "I may say I don't believe in gushing much in these College Biog's and think a dryer statement much fitter."

In his college friendships Wendell was attracted by colorful personalities and stimulating conversation. Though deeply interested in philosophy and art, he did not shut his eyes to the approaching struggle between North and South. Slavery was repugnant to his sense of elementary fairness as well as to his religious feelings. "Do men own any other men by God's law?" he asked himself. He joined a group of young men who took upon themselves the duty of protecting abolitionist speakers from the possible fury of audiences that might get out of hand. A note written him by a friend during this period reads: "I do hope you will not receive personal injury tomorrow and trust you will not use a weapon save as a last resort."

In later life he admitted that the inexorable drift to war created in him the conviction that man's life was necessarily linked with struggle, suffering, and pain. The coming war posed a personal challenge to him, and the only honorable answer to the challenge was to volunteer. For, as he was to say later, "Life is action and passion. I think it is required of a man that he should share the action and passion of his time at peril of being judged not to have lived."

At the time of the 1860 election, Wendell was still eighteen months short of voting age; but right after Lincoln's inauguration at the beginning of March, 1861, he enlisted in the Union army. His military training started two months before graduation. Like most members of the Class of '61, he would continue his education on some of the bloodiest battlefields of the Civil War.

What the young man saw and experienced during the war made him forever after impatient of all sham and pretense. Equally unforgettable was the impression created by what a later writer was to call "grace under pressure." This is perhaps best illustrated by a remarkable passage from a Memorial Day address Holmes delivered in 1884—he was talking about a wartime friend, Major Henry L. Abbott:

"His few surviving companions will never forget the awful spectacle of his advance alone with his company in the streets of Fredericksburg. In less than sixty seconds he would become the focus of a hidden and annihilating fire from a semicircle of houses. His first platoon had vanished under it in an instant, ten men falling dead by his side. He had quietly turned back to where the other half of his company was waiting, had given the order, 'Second platoon, forward!' and was again moving on, in obedience to superior command, to certain and useless death, when the order he was obeying was countermanded. The end was distant only a few seconds; but if you had seen him with his indifferent carriage, and sword swinging from his finger like a cane, you would never have suspected that he was doing more than conducting a company drill on the camp parade ground."

But at the beginning of his service such scenes were mercifully hidden from him. After his unit had gone south but before it had seen combat, he could still write jaunty notes to his mother about "the organized boredom" of war:

"It's a campaign now & no mistake— No tents, no trunks—no nothing—it has rained like the devil last night all day and tonight and you may guess what the mud is in a clayey soil where it was a real annoyance before— Marching will have to be slow for the roads have constantly to be made or mended for the artillery. . . ." And he concludes by describing an all-day march, up to his knees in mud.

His baptism in battle came at Ball's Bluff in Septem-

ber, 1861. (By this time he had been promoted to lieutenant.) The terrain was very unfavorable for the
Union forces and they were poorly led. The result was
a catastrophic defeat, with heavy casualties. Holmes took
a bullet in the chest which barely missed his heart and
lungs. For a while the doctors were uncertain of his
recovery, but he was soon out of danger. After three
weeks he was sent to Philadelphia, where his father met
him, still pale and weak, and took him home.

Under his mother's loving care, the wound gradually
healed and Holmes grew more cheerful and once more
eager for company. Eight months after being wounded,
he rejoined his regiment in Virginia. He was now a
captain. War was marching for twelve hours under a
broiling sun, making a bayonet charge in knee-deep
mud, going without food for thirty hours, and sleeping
in the rain. The rest was boredom, with sudden death
lurking on every side. "Shall I confess a frightful fact?"
he writes his mother. "Many of the officers including
your beloved son have discovered themselves to have
been attacked by body lice. . . ."

Sixty years later he could still recall vividly the hardships of those days: "I remember just before the battle
of Antietam thinking and perhaps saying to a brother
officer that it would be easy after a comfortable break-
fast to come down the steps of one's house pulling on
one's gloves and smoking a cigar, to get on to a horse
and charge a battery up Beacon Street, while the ladies
wave handkerchiefs from a balcony. But the reality was
to pass a night on the ground in the rain with your
bowels out of order and then after no particular break-

fast to wade a stream and attack the enemy. That is life."

At Antietam he was shot through the neck; the bullet narrowly missed the windpipe and jugular vein. An army doctor, concluding from the location of the wound that the stricken man could not last much longer, was about to move on to other patients when a fellow officer insisted that Holmes be given a more careful examination. Accordingly the doctor studied the wound and finally decided that Holmes had a chance to recover after all. In fact, he was back with the army within two months.

But soon after his return Holmes was again wounded, this time by shrapnel that shattered a foot. It took him almost nine months to recover this time, but the wound was to trouble him for the rest of his life. He returned to active service in 1864 as a staff officer; he had been promoted to lieutenant colonel, partly because he was a valued officer and partly because so many of his contemporaries had been killed. Of the twenty lieutenants he had known at the beginning of the war, fifteen were gone. Many years were to pass before he could look back to those grim years and sum them up in these words: "Through our great good fortune, in our youth our hearts were touched with fire. It was given to us to learn at the outset that life is a profound and passionate thing."

After he was released from military service, he had to choose a profession. Literature, philosophy, and etching all fascinated him, but in none of these was he outstanding. His choice of a law career baffled his friends; as he later asked, "How can the laborious study of a dry and technical system, the greedy watch for clients and practice of shopkeepers' arts, the mannerless conflicts over often sordid interests, make out a life?"

That was one way of looking at a legal career. But there was another aspect: "In what other does one plunge so deep in the stream of life—so share its passions, its battles, its despair, its triumphs, both as witness and actor?" And it may well be that the wartime carnage he had just lived through had something to do with his choice.

For while the law has many aspects, its most important one is making decisions possible without resort to force. How well do legal systems work? How do they develop historically? How do they prove adequate or inadequate to solve the problems of each age? Why do they sometimes break down? What happens when they break down? Perhaps this last question was his first: the Civil War had showed him what happens when a legal system proves inadequate to solve the burning problem of the age.

After studying law for two years, Holmes was admitted to the bar in 1867. He continued his researches into the law so intensively that despite his youth he came to be recognized as an outstanding authority; in 1870 Harvard appointed him to teach constitutional law. He had begun to contribute articles to law journals which were admired for their acute reasoning, their learning, their lucid presentation.

Though Holmes worked hard in those early years,

most people thought of him as fortune's favorite. He wrote and spoke beautifully; he was always the master of the flashing phrase. He was likable yet set apart; he was affable but distinctively himself. And he knew how to disagree without hurting his opponent's feelings.

In 1872 Holmes married Fanny Bowditch Dixwell. At thirty-one he was still unable to earn a substantial living, and the young couple had to live with his parents. The usual in-law relationship was reversed, for Fanny got on famously with her husband's parents and served as a buffer between Wendell and his father.

Dr. Holmes despised the law as a career and was often tactless in his comments on his son's studies; he saw no point in continuing them. The son, stung by these disparaging remarks, immediately took offense; and on each of these occasions it was up to Mrs. Holmes senior and Mrs. Holmes junior to keep the peace. Dr. Holmes described his generous and warm-hearted daughter-in-law as "a very helpful, hopeful, powerful as well as brilliant woman." With all her incisive intelligence she was self-effacing, self-sacrificing, and uncomplaining. Her companionable qualities and keen sense of humor helped to ease the strain that is the natural lot of every conscientious judge. Their marriage of almost sixty years' duration was a very happy one, marred only by the lack of children.

After several years Holmes was offered a partnership in one of Boston's leading law firms, and the young couple were at last able to move into their own apartment. But legal practice was not the solution for

Holmes; in fact, it bored him. His approach to law was scholarly: he was fascinated by the study of the English common law—the unwritten law developed by custom and by court decisions over many centuries and then taken over into American law.

Studying long into the night, Holmes traced the origins of the common law in the customs of the Germanic tribes in ancient times. He followed the development of the common law as it was adjusted to the needs of succeeding ages. He showed how provisions of the common law had evolved out of conflicts and then —as the conditions of social and economic life had gradually changed—had become useless, even harmful. Where the law did change, it did so belatedly, with a considerable lag.

So far this was all theory, suitable for a cloistered scholar. But Holmes was not afraid "to think for action upon which great interests depend." Theory meant nothing to him if it did not have an application here and now. He therefore concluded: "The present has a right to govern itself so far as it can; and it ought always to be remembered that historic continuity with the past is not a duty, it is only a necessity."

The lawyers and judges of his day were outraged. To them the law was majestic, perfect, and eternal; to tell them that the law had to be changed to adapt it to changing times and institutions, made them feel that the earth was trembling under their feet. The Founding Fathers, in writing the Constitution, had provided for amendments because they realized that succeeding generations would live under conditions that would call

for changes in the Constitution or additions to it. Yet
Holmes's contemporaries could not appreciate the sound
good sense of his argument.

Legal decisions, they had always believed, were based
on precedent. And once a precedent was established,
it was to stand forever. Men were always to do thus and
so because their ancestors had done thus and so. Imagine
their indignation when they read these daring words
written by a highly respectable young man in the quiet
of his study:

"The law embodies the story of a nation's development through many centuries, and it cannot be dealt
with as if it contained only the axioms and corollaries
of a book of mathematics." Holmes was saying, in effect,
that a law had to be appraised in terms of its adequacy
to solve the problems that had brought it into existence
and the problems to which it was currently being applied.

Even more disagreeable was this bombshell: "The life
of the law has not been logic: it has been experience.
The felt necessities of the time, the prevalent moral and
political theories, intuitions of public policy, avowed or
unconscious, even the prejudices that judges share with
their fellow men, have had a great deal more to do than
the syllogism in determining the rules by which men
should be governed." Here Holmes was realistically
pointing out that the passage and interpretation of
laws are strongly influenced by personal attitudes and
passionate political conflicts. These two sentences were
to lay the basis for the famous Supreme Court dissents
of Holmes's later years.

These opinions were embodied in a notable book, *The Common Law,* which Holmes published in 1881. It featured precisely the kind of scholarship—original, fearless, and far-reaching—that Emerson had called for in his famous address, *The American Scholar.* So powerful was the impression made by his hard-headed arguments that even those who were unconvinced nevertheless respected him. There was a growing conviction that the next vacancy in the Massachusetts Supreme Court would be offered to him, despite the fact that he had never served as a judge.

One of the few who appreciated Holmes was Louis Dembitz Brandeis, fifteen years Holmes's junior but his equal as a brilliant student of the law. The two men, despite the dissimilarity of their backgrounds and their approach to the law, took an instant liking to each other. Holmes's Puritan ancestors had come to Massachusetts in the seventeenth century to escape from Stuart tyranny. Brandeis' freedom-loving family had come to America in 1848, the year when liberalism was crushed in many European countries.

From his parents the young Brandeis had acquired a deep love of culture, a lasting faith in American institutions, and a burning conviction that it was the function of the law to right existing wrongs. But instead of the historical method favored by Holmes, Brandeis used the method of thoroughgoing factual analysis. "If you can't solve it by law," he was fond of saying, "you can solve it by mathematics." Both men saw eye to eye in their belief that law has to change to deal adequately with the problems of each new generation.

After almost sixty years of friendship, Holmes was to write, "In moments of discouragement that we all pass through, Brandeis has always had the happy word that lifts one's heart. It came from knowledge, experience, courage and the high way in which he has always taken life. Whenever he left my house I was likely to say to my wife, 'There goes a really good man.' " After Brandeis' appointment to the Supreme Court in 1914, the phrase "Justices Holmes and Brandeis dissenting" was to become familiar even to people who took no interest in public affairs.

In 1882, while the impact of his book was still fresh, Holmes was appointed to the Massachusetts Supreme Court. He became Chief Justice in 1896 and served until 1902. America was changing rapidly from a predominantly agricultural economy to a predominantly industrial economy; old laws were becoming dangerously outmoded because of their inability to meet new problems.

Holmes had used a telling phrase about "the felt necessities of the time." As a judge, he saw it as his duty to put the new necessities into words—into law. Production methods were becoming highly specialized. As industrial plants multiplied, more and more immigrants were needed from Europe. The farmer was finding it ever more difficult to get a living from a small acreage, to buy the most efficient machinery, to keep up with his bank loans. Great industrial combines were steadily growing larger, and labor unrest and the removal of competition were creating problems that existing laws could not solve.

Much of the popular discontent centered on Supreme Court decisions dealing with the right of Congress to regulate interstate commerce, granted by the Constitution. Liberals felt that this clause gave Congress the power to remedy existing evils by passing appropriate laws.

Conservatives, on the other hand, relied on the Fourteenth Amendment, passed in 1866 to protect the civil rights of the newly freed Negroes. "No State," the amendment reads, "shall deprive any person of life, liberty, or property without due process of law." Since in the eyes of the law a corporation is a "person," the amendment came to be used as a protection for corporations whenever any state passed a law affecting corporations.

Holmes well knew how words could be used with what he shrewdly called "delusive exactness." As he put it in one of his opinions, "A word is not a crystal, transparent and unchanged; it is the skin of a living thought and may vary greatly in color and content according to the circumstances and time in which it is used." The change in the meaning of "person" is a perfect example.

For a long time Holmes tried as hard as he could to reconcile himself to the legal reasoning of the day. In his first seven years in the Massachusetts Supreme Court, he dissented only twice from the majority opinions. He first attracted nation-wide attention in 1896 with his dissent in the case of Vogelahn vs. Guntner in which he upheld the right of peaceful picketing. His position was a lonely one, for although he upheld the right of labor unions to organize, he made it clear that he was dubious about the benefits they might achieve.

Yet the members of his profession thought of him as a radical. It made them uncomfortable to read the courageous dissenting opinion, with such observations as these: "One of the eternal conflicts out of which life is made up is that between the effort of every man to get the most he can for his services, and that of society, disguised under the name of capital, to get his services for the least possible return. Combination on the one side is patent and powerful. Combination on the other is the necessary and desirable counterpart, if the battle is to be carried on in a fair and equal way."

Holmes had become such a distinguished figure that when a vacancy occurred in the Supreme Court in 1902 he was appointed to fill the post. He was now sixty-two years old, an age at which most people are getting ready for retirement instead of looking forward to starting a career.

"It is a good deal of a wrench," Holmes told his admirers at a dinner given in his honor, "to leave old friends. But, gentlemen, it is a great adventure, and that thought brings with it a mighty joy. To have one's chance to do one's share in shaping the laws of the whole country spreads over one the hush that one used to feel when awaiting the beginning of a battle." But even Holmes could hardly have foreseen that his most important and most fruitful achievements lay ahead of him.

It soon became clear that Holmes did not see eye to eye with the majority of the court. Justice Sutherland expressed the majority view in somewhat extreme form when he said:

"There is nothing more unfortunate in governmental administration than a policy of playing fast and loose with great economic and political principles which have . . . become part of our fundamental wisdom. . . . Conditions may change, but the principle itself is immutable; once righteous, it is always righteous." This was the theory that Holmes had demolished over twenty years earlier in *The Common Law*.

Holmes on the other hand maintained that a judge must be able to reconcile himself to the disappearance of much that he holds dear—as long as it is "done away with short of revolution by the orderly change of law." In his very first year on the court he made clear his advocacy of "judicial restraint"—his view that a judge must strive to keep his personal likes and dislikes out of his decisions. "It by no means is true that every law is void which may seem to the judges who pass upon it excessive, unsuited to its ostensible end, or based upon conceptions of morality with which they disagree."

Holmes was thoroughly convinced that the Constitution gave Congress and the states scope to deal with such contemporary problems as child labor and maximum working hours. For if the Constitution was not applicable in such matters, then there existed a vacuum in which government could not function. Life was a conflict, he had often said, and the law that reflected the realities of the living process should allow a fair field to all.

Usually his dissents took the form of delectable irony, but sometimes he lost patience and a sharper tone crept into them. In one case he informed the majority that the provisions of the Constitution were not "mathematical formulas"; their significance was "to be gathered not simply by taking the words and a dictionary, but by considering their origin and the line of their growth."

The fact that Holmes's reputation on the court was made with his famous dissents is somewhat deceptive. Invariably he dissented reluctantly because he felt that dissents damaged the dignity of the court and hurt the confidence of the people in their government. As a matter of fact, his dissents were far fewer than those of his colleagues. But it was the importance of the issues involved, and the distinguished quality of his dissenting opinions, that gave them their popular interest and enduring fame.

When the New York State Legislature passed a law in 1905 limiting the hours of work in bakeries to not more than ten a day or sixty a week, the Supreme Court held the law unconstitutional by a vote of 5 to 4. This was the famous Lochner case, which evoked one of Holmes's most powerful and memorable dissents. In the course of time Holmes's view was the one that prevailed; many of his other dissents had the same fate.

Holmes was strongly convinced that the state law

was perfectly constitutional; hence his pointed rebuke to the court majority:

"A constitution is not intended to embody a particular theory. . . . It is made for people of fundamentally differing views, and the accident of our finding certain opinions natural and familiar or novel and even shocking ought not to conclude our judgment upon the question whether statutes embodying them conflict with the Constitution of the United States." He tried hard to live up to this recommendation in his own rulings, upholding laws that seemed "futile or even noxious to me and to those whose judgment I most respect."

Holmes's impish sense of humor often baffled his fellow justices. On one occasion he was reading an opinion representing the views of the majority. It was a formidable document, bristling with learned references, statistical tables, footnotes, committee reports and the like. Holmes, then seventy-eight, wrote in the space reserved for his opinion: "This afternoon I was walking on the towpath and saw a cardinal. It seemed to me to be the first sign of Spring. By the way, I concur."

If any humorless colleague suspected that Holmes was too old for court work, he was set right by another opinion written in the same year. When an Arizona copper miner sued his employer to recover for injuries incurred on the job, the Supreme Court upheld the employer by a 5–4 majority. To Holmes it seemed a shabby thing that the employee could obtain no redress for his injuries.

Yet there is nothing sentimental about Holmes's com-

ment. In fact, we get the impression that he deliberately
set himself to show that he could be just as hard-headed
as the other justices and come to diametrically opposite conclusions:

"If a business is unsuccessful," he wrote, "it means
that the public does not care enough for it to make it
pay. If it is successful the public pays its expenses and
something more. It is reasonable that the public should
pay the whole cost of producing what it wants and a
part of that cost is the pain and mutilation incident
to production. By throwing that loss upon the employer in the first instance we throw it upon the public
in the long run and that is just."

It was also in this year (1919) that civil liberties
cases arising from the Espionage Act passed during
World War I began to reach the Supreme Court.
Steeped as he was in the American traditions of free
speech and a free press, Holmes was deeply troubled
about this repressive law and its rather harsh penalties.
"I have had to deal with cases," he wrote a friend,
"that made my blood boil and yet seemed to create no
feeling in the public or even in most of my brethren."

In the Abrams case the Supreme Court upheld the
conviction of several men who had printed and distributed leaflets attacking the United States war effort
against Germany and asking for opposition to any
American intervention in the Russian civil wars. Under
the Esponiage Act they were convicted and sentenced
to twenty years' imprisonment.

Holmes despised their political views—"a creed that I believe to be the creed of ignorance and immaturity." But he felt that the sentence was much too harsh. In any event these "poor and puny anonymities," as he contemptuously described them, deserved the protection of the First Amendment—"Congress shall make no law . . . abridging the freedom of speech." Holmes realized that in wartime the right to speak freely has to be restrained to some extent because "war opens dangers that do not exist at other times."

To meet this problem, Holmes devised the rule of "clear and present danger." No one, he said, had a right to cry "Fire!" in a crowded theater. Similarly, the authorities had the right to guard the national welfare against abuses of free speech in a time of great crisis. But, he concluded, a more lenient view should be taken of such cases where there was little or no danger of serious consequences.

In the Rosika Schwimmer case of 1929, when Holmes was eighty-eight years old, he again took a far more enlightened view than the court majority. Miss Schwimmer, who had been disqualified from acquiring citizenship because she was an avowed pacifist, fought the decision up to the Supreme Court, which decided against her. During the course of the hearings Mrs. Holmes died, and the aged Justice was so broken with grief that he at first held out against a public funeral. If he had excused himself from participation in the case no one would have taken it amiss. But the sense of public duty was still as keen in him as it had been at Antietam and

Chancellorsville. His dissent in the Schwimmer case ranks among his greatest. Of Miss Schwimmer's patriotism he wrote:

"So far as the adequacy of her oath is concerned, I hardly can see how that is affected by the statement, inasmuch as she is a woman over fifty years of age, and would not be allowed to bear arms if she wanted to."

Holmes made it clear that he emphatically disagreed with Miss Schwimmer's views. But this disagreement had no effect on his thinking about the legal merits of the case: "Some of her answers might excite popular prejudice, but if there is any principle of the Constitution that more imperatively calls for attachment than any other, it is the principle of free thought—not free thought for those who agree with us but freedom for the thought that we hate."

As Justice Holmes approached the end of his amazingly long career, he sometimes wondered whether it had all been worth while. After half a century on the bench, he had nothing to show but hundreds of opinions, some on trivial matters. Was that all there was to the law? He imagined Shakespeare saying, "Yes, I have written five thousand lines of solid gold and a good deal of padding—I, who would have covered the Milky Way with words that outshone the stars!" But he did not lose heart: "We cannot live our dreams. We are lucky enough if we can give a sample of our best, and if in our hearts we can feel that it has been nobly done."

Each year the most promising student of the graduating class of Harvard Law School was given the honor of serving as clerk to the Justice. These young men, known as Holmes's "Annuals," had very little work to do. They provided the old man with companionship, balanced his checkbook, paid his bills, enjoyed his jokes, and incidentally obtained a priceless understanding of the ideas and working habits of a very great man.

In his eighties, his home was a gathering place for some of the most brilliant men in Washington—all of them a good deal younger than himself, of course. Sometimes, returning from a tiring court session, he would arrive in the middle of a heated argument. Eagerly he would ask, "What is it? Tell me, I'll take the opposite side."

Reading Morison's *History of the United States* at the age of eighty-eight, he commented to a friend, "He made me recognize prejudices of my own." How many younger people would be capable of this reaction?

Two years later, on his ninetieth birthday, he spoke for the first time on the radio. Deeply moved by the tributes that poured in from all parts of the country and from Europe, he had heard Chief Justice Hughes conclude his welcoming speech with these words: "We honor him, but, what is more, we love him. We give him tonight the homage of our hearts."

"The race is over," Holmes said in his reply, "but the work never is done while the power to work still remains." A month later, as the apple trees bloomed and the magnolias came out, he was writing, "I want to idle and take in the Spring, but it may not be."

A year later he submitted his resignation from the

court. His mind was just as alert as ever, but he was no longer strong enough to carry the burden. After his retirement, he devoted much of his remaining time to books. In many cases the authors were men whose ideas were not to his taste, but his mind still flourished on discussion, opposition, the clash of contending views. He never lost his faith in the triumph of truth in the market place of ideas.

When Holmes wanted his secretary to read to him he would say, "Let's have a little self-improvement, Sonny." For life, even life at ninety, was always growth, striving for self-improvement. When President Franklin Delano Roosevelt visited him in 1933 after his inauguration, the old man was reading Plato.

"Why do you read Plato, Mr. Justice?"

"To improve my mind, Mr. President."

The President had just closed the banks. Fear stalked the land. For all his jaunty air the President was deeply troubled. Just before leaving, he said to Holmes, "You have lived through half our country's history; you have seen its great men. This is a dark hour. Justice Holmes, what is your advice to me?"

"You are in a war, Mr. President. I was in a war, too. And in a war there is only one rule: *Form your battalions and fight.*"

He died two weeks before his ninety-fourth birthday. At the conclusion of the funeral services the officiating minister added this quotation from Justice Holmes:

"We accept our destiny to work, to fight, to die for ideal aims. At the grave of a hero who has done these things, we end, not with sorrow at the inevitable loss, but with the contagion of his courage; and with a kind of desperate joy we go back to the fight."

These are noble words, inspiring words. They remind us that when Adams, the "Old Man Eloquent," fought the Gag Rule, when Mann strove to lift his fellow citizens from brutish ignorance, when Garrison struck his hammer blows at the shame of slavery, when Emerson and Thoreau wrote and spoke to liberate men from their self-imposed servitude, and when Holmes, year after weary year, with one friend, or none, at his side, wrote his great dissents, they kept alive a noble ideal.

In 1787, when the representatives of the several states gathered to "form a more perfect union, they gave men the feeling that something good, something great, had come into the world." If that feeling still remains with us, we have the Great Dissenters to thank for its preservation.

When Justice Holmes's will was read, it was revealed that the bulk of his estate, amounting to about $250,000, had been bequeathed to the United States Government. It was an eloquent gesture, expressive of his lifelong love for his country and its people; yet it was not half so eloquent of that love as the great dissents.

BIBLIOGRAPHY

James Truslow Adams, *The Adams Family*. Boston: Little, Brown & Company, 1930.

————, *New England in the Republic, 1776–1850*. Boston: Little, Brown & Company, 1927.

J. Brooks Atkinson, *Henry Thoreau, The Cosmic Yankee*. New York: Alfred A. Knopf, Inc., 1927.

Samuel Flagg Bemis, *John Quincy Adams and the Foundations of American Foreign Policy*. New York: Alfred A. Knopf, Inc., 1949.

————, *John Quincy Adams and the Union*. New York: Alfred A. Knopf, Inc., 1956.

Silas Bent, *Justice Oliver Wendell Holmes*. New York: The Vanguard Press, Inc., 1932.

Francis Biddle, *Mr. Justice Holmes*. New York: Charles Scribner's Sons, 1943.

Catherine Drinker Bowen, *Yankee from Olympus*. Boston: Little, Brown & Company, 1944.

Van Wyck Brooks, *The Flowering of New England*. New York: E. P. Dutton & Company, 1940.

Henry Seidel Canby, *Thoreau: a Biography*. Boston: Houghton Mifflin Company, 1939.

Bennett Champ Clark, *John Quincy Adams*. Boston: Little, Brown & Company, 1932.

W. P. Garrison, *William Lloyd Garrison, 1805–1879.* Boston: Houghton Mifflin Company, 1894.

George Allen Hibbell, *Horace Mann, Educator, Patriot, and Reformer.* Philadelphia: William F. Fell Company, 1910.

B. A. Hinsdale, *Horace Mann and the Common School Revival in the United States.* New York: Charles Scribner's Sons, 1900.

Mark DeWolfe Howe (editor), *Holmes-Pollock Letters.* Cambridge: Harvard University Press, 1941.

————, *The Shaping Years.* Cambridge: The Belknap Press of Harvard University, 1957.

———— (editor), *Touched with Fire.* Cambridge: Harvard University Press, 1947.

Ralph Korngold, *Two Friends of Man.* Boston: Little, Brown & Company, 1950.

Max Lerner (editor), *The Mind and Faith of Justice Holmes.* Garden City, N.Y.: Halcyon House, 1948.

George A. Lipsky, *John Quincy Adams: His Theory and Ideas.* New York: Thomas Y. Crowell Company, 1950.

Joy Elmer Morgan, *Horace Mann: His Ideas and Ideals.* Washington, D.C.: National Home Library Foundation, 1937.

Allan Nevins (editor), *The Diary of John Quincy Adams, 1794–1845.* New York: Longmans, Green and Company, Inc., 1928.

Russel B. Nye, *William L. Garrison and the Humanitarian Reformers*. Boston: Little, Brown & Company, 1955.

Bliss Perry, *The Heart of Emerson's Journals*. Boston: Houghton Mifflin Company, 1926.

Ralph L. Rusk, *The Life of Ralph Waldo Emerson*. New York: Charles Scribner's Sons, 1949.

Philips Russell, *Emerson, the Wisest American*. New York: Brentano's, Inc., 1929.

L. M. Tharp, *Until Victory*. Boston: Little, Brown & Company, 1953.

Henry David Thoreau, *Walden and Other Writings*. New York: Random House, 1937.

Bradford Torrey and Francis H. Allen (editors), *The Journal of Henry D. Thoreau*. Boston: Houghton Mifflin Company, 1906.

E. I. Williams, *Horace Mann, Educational Statesman*. New York: The Macmillan Company, 1937.

INDEX

ABOUT THE AUTHOR

Fred Reinfeld was born in, and has always lived in or around, New York. At one time or another in his life he has been an accountant, chess-master, bookseller, and instructor. Working and playing in chess tournaments has taken him all over the United States. He has written on a wide variety of subjects, including chess, stamp collecting, coin collecting, geology, atomic energy, and the great inventions of the world.

From earliest childhood Mr. Reinfeld was fascinated by American history, and read voluminously in this field. As he grew older, he determined to present a picture of men who were not afraid to take the unpopular side on important questions of principle and did not shrink from the laborious task of stirring Americans to an awareness of their rights as individuals. *The Great Dissenters* is the result of this lifetime interest in American history.

DATE DUE
